Moral Education for the Emotionally Disturbed Early Adolescent

Moral Education for the Emotionally Disturbed Early Adolescent

An Application of Kohlbergian Techniques and Spiritual Principles

Eileen Marie Gardner

LexingtonBooks
D.C. Heath and Company
Lexington, Massachusetts
Toronto

Library of Congress Cataloging in Publication Data

Gardner, Eileen Marie.
    Moral education for the emotionally disturbed early adolescent.

    Bibliography: p. 185
    Includes index.
    1. Moral education—Philosophy.   2. Mentally ill
children—Education—Curricula.   3. Adolescence.
I. Title.
LC268.G33 1983   371.94   82–49250
ISBN 0–669–06448–3

Copyright © 1983 by D.C. Heath and Company

Published simultaneously in Canada

Printed in the United States of America

International Standard Book Number: 0–669–06448–3

Library of Congress Catalog Card Number: 82–49250

*To my family
with special indebtedness
to my mother
with whom I collaborated closely
in the writing of my philosophy*

Contents

Preface

During the 1978–1979 academic year this author applied a specific educational program to a group of severely emotionally disturbed early adolescents. This program was an amalgamation of three teaching approaches: Kohlbergian moral education, this author's philosophy, and behavior modification.

Five of the previous six years had been spent by this researcher in teaching severely disturbed and learning-disabled children aged eight to thirteen. She had finally succeeded in developing an effective academic and affective-educational program: significant gains in academic skills were attained by most of her students, and gross behavior problems were brought under control.

Some of the students, however, who lived in particularly difficult home environments, were not sufficiently affected by the teaching methods applied to them. Short-term gains were eclipsed by deeply entrenched disturbed thinking and behavior. These students seemed lost within confusing life situations over which they were unable to exert control.

This author's desire to reach these students led her to inquire about other teaching methods—methods to help disturbed children take the broader view, understand where they fit within the larger whole, and direct their lives accordingly. She wished to identify the type of classroom atmosphere and program that would have lasting beneficial results in modifying the reasoning, behavior, academic achievement, and ability to cope with disturbing life situations of severely disturbed early adolescents.

Eventually this teacher heard about the work of Lawrence Kohlberg and moral education. After spending one year at Harvard University studying Dr. Kohlberg's theory, she returned to her teaching job and included his educational approach in her already established program. Kohlbergian moral education was applied to a group of disturbed early adolescents because the teacher/researcher wished to test the ability of this educational approach to help emotionally disturbed children take control of their uncontrolled lives through the practice of rational decision making (the basis of Kohlbergian moral education).

This book is a report on the effect of the expanded program on the afore-mentioned group of emotionally disturbed children.

Any substantive educational program must rest on a firm philosophical foundation. For this reason chapter 1 details the philosophies of Plato (one foundation of this author's philosophy and highly relevant to the techniques of Kohlbergian moral education), of Kant and Rawls (from whom Kohlberg drew), of Kohlberg, and of this author; discusses their points of agreement and disagreement; and finally (within this author's philosophy) weighs the relative merits of their basic assumptions. Chapter 2 describes the application of the three approaches previously mentioned to the class of emotionally disturbed early adolescents, the school in which the experimental class was housed, and the core seven students. Chapter 3, the central chapter of the book, is a narrative analysis of the interaction between the students and the educational program applied to them. Chapter 4 presents the conclusions. Appendixes providing specific test scores and other background data complete the work. All names used throughout this book are fictitious.

1 Philosophy

Plato

Plato espoused a theory that has been labeled "rational intuitionism."[1] It is rational in that man must use his intellect in his effort to grasp eternal and absolute truths upon which this world is modeled; it is intuitionist in that those truths represent seed (intuitive) knowledge in man that must be "called out" to be objectively known. This calling out is accomplished through the exercise of the rational mind.

The Forms

Rational intuitionism rests on the assumption that basic moral concepts such as the right, the good, and the just are not analyzable by nonmoral concepts; they are, rather, self-evident propositions or principles independent of the natural world. Natural man can recall these concepts, Plato argues, because he once belonged to the world in which they reside. A significant segment of Plato's writings is devoted to his attempt to prove by rational argument that man knows "the good," not because there is a true example of it on the material plane, which there is not, but because his soul (as immaterial and distinct from the body) has originated in and will return to a place of purity where eternal moral truths reside.[2]

These eternal moral truths Plato calls the "forms." They are the antecedent causes of all that is found in the physical world, and in being so, become the objective standards by which all else is measured. Learning is a recollection of the forms: when a person claims that two sticks are equal, for instance, he does not mean that they are so in an absolute sense. No two sticks can be absolutely equal in this world; there will always be something unlike about them, says Plato. Yet, a person uses the term *equality* when referring to two sticks that are very similar because, Plato argues, he has at some time experienced true equality. Since he cannot have experienced true equality in this world, the individual must have experienced it in another and must be recollecting that experience when he sees a thing that possesses its characteristics in this one.[3]

1

This is true, not only for the absolute standard of equality, but for all absolute standards.

In summary, the forms "move beyond" ordinary belief (which is changing and mutable) to that which is fixed in what Plato calls the "real" nature of things and therefore, immutable. They are unchanging, single, of the same essence, pure, clear, and remote from the physical world.

Cognitive States

The aim of human development is to ascend to the lofty region where the forms reside and there to perceive the reality of things. Plato compares the individual's journey to the heights to a man emerging from a state of darkness, unreality, and ignorance into a state of the light of the real and the true. He divides these two states (darkness and light) into two sections each, thereby producing what he calls the four cognitive states. The first two cognitive states—imagination and confidence—correspond to the soul in the dark without the form of the good. The second two—thought and intelligence—correspond to the soul in the light, aware of the good and looking at the forms.[4] Plato argues that the individual soul or groups of souls can be characterized at any particular time by one of these four cognitive states and that the order of these states, from imagination to confidence to thought to intelligence, is a map of the cognitive progression of the developing soul. This progression also may be considered to represent different conditions of moral belief at different stages of moral education. Plato tells what is called "the Cave Allegory," summarized in the following paragraphs, to describe the progression.

The first cognitive state, called imagination, conjecture, or picture thought, Plato likens to the life of men dwelling as prisoners in a subterranean cavern, who take shadows to be reality. At this unenlightened stage man is a prisoner shackled in semidarkness to a childlike perception of reality, unable to examine what he is perceiving.

Imagine next, Plato asks, an individual who has been freed from his fetters in the cavern and who is able for the first time to walk about and to examine his world in a greater light. He approaches the entrance to the cave, but the clear light of the sun is painful and blinding to his eyes. The neophyte mistrusts and is confused by his new perceptions. He wishes, perhaps, to return to his former state of bondage. But once freed, this the neophyte cannot do. He is forced to use a previously untapped resource—his reason—to assimilate the new information and to differentiate the true from what has formerly only seemed true. This state, called confidence, is an important one in the progression of the soul from ignorance to knowledge in that it marks man's first opportunity to use his mind.

The third cognitive state, called thought or understanding, is likened to a man emerged from the cave and standing in a world lit by sunlight (truth). No longer is he shackled by the illusions of the cavern; no longer is he blinded by the sun as in his first emergence. Accustomed to this new world, he becomes aware of the forms (which preside over all things in the visible region) and he uses his reason to achieve knowledge of them.

This new-found awareness so totally transforms the person that he is deaf to enticements to return to his former state of bondage and shadow; he pities those who still dwell therein. If he were to return, so altered would he seem to his former comrades that they, in their ignorance, would take his rebirth as a sign of madness and would fear the ascent which had so transformed him.

This third cognitive state, thought, is not considered the highest because of the method it uses to investigate the nature of reality: instead of ascending to first principles to clarify the world of the senses, the individual at this state manipulates conventional hypotheses consistent with ordinary beliefs. The error lies in his believing that assumptions based on ordinary beliefs are accurate indicators of truth instead of what they really are—mere springboards to the ideas that transcend them.

The last and highest cognitive state Plato calls intelligence or science. It rests on a set of beliefs that are drawn from first principles. While the individual at this level uses hypotheses to investigate the nature of the forms, these hypotheses are not considered to be absolutes but mere vehicles to reaching the pure forms which "require no assumption and [are] the starting point of all." Once the thinker has entered the world of the true and the good where realities (or forms) can be apprehended "only by the mind," he is free to move systematically from idea to idea, making no use whatsoever of any object of sense.[5]

Order in the Soul and in the State

Plato places great emphasis on what he calls the "three parts of a man's soul." These parts and their ordering form a basis for the organization of a state, the education of its citizenry, and Plato's definition of justice. In ascending order these parts are the appetitive, the "thumos" or high spirited, and the reason.

The appetitive part of man includes nutrition and generation—food, drink, sex, getting warm. It also includes the money-loving part, as money is the chief instrument by which the appetites are gratified. This, the lowest part of man, represents his instinctive animal nature, his brute urges without conceptualization, his blind, unintellectualized desires. It is distinct in its inability to govern itself or to set limits on its activity. It is insatiable. When gratified, the appetitive part grows and takes over, bending the other two parts to its will. Because the appetitive part inherently lacks reason and moderation, its capacity for distortion is boundless. Therefore, man must use his reason to control it.

The "thumos" or high-spirited part of man includes the emotions—anger, joy, fear, disgust. It is the ambitious part that is covetous of honor, predominance, victory, and good repute. In the well-nurtured soul, Plato argues, the thumos becomes reason's ally and fights without quarter for the just.

The highest part of the soul is reason. It embraces the rational, calculative, and intellectual part of man. The reason is most concerned with the truth of things and least concerned with wealth and reputation. It is self-sufficient, free of the unbridled impulses of the appetitive desires and of the self-aggrandizement urges of the thumos. It is the source of motivation which helps man to choose the correct course in life. It is pure, orderly, harmonious, true, and precise. Not surprisingly, reason rules most strongly in the soul of the lover of learning and the lover of wisdom.[6]

Plato claims that the excellence of the human soul lies in its consistency and structure, which is the reflection of a geometrical order in the universe ("kosmos"). That order places the reason first, the thumos second, and the appetites last in the human soul. The higher parts must rule the lower. If this order is maintained, each part is able to do that for which it is best suited. If this order is upset and the lower parts rule where the highest should, the highest is then either constrained to pursue an "alien pleasure" or is delegated to inactivity. If this is allowed to happen, the soul becomes filled with inner dissension and is lost in the senseless muck of the unreal:

> Then those who have no experience of wisdom and virtue . . . are swept downward . . . and back again to the center, and so sway and roam to and fro . . . but they have never transcended all this and turned their eyes to the true upper region . . . nor ever been really filled with real things, nor ever tasted stable and pure pleasure, but with their eyes ever bent upon the earth and heads bowed down over their tables . . . feast like cattle, grazing and copulating, ever greedy for more of these delights . . . they slay one another in stateless avidity, . . . vainly striving to satisfy with things that are not the real—the unreal and incontinent part of their souls.[7]

The soul secures immunity from its desires only under the tutelage of reason. Reason rules by virtue of its contemplation of the forms (the true, the divine, the unconjecturable), its ability to draw inspiration from them, and its ability to plan and to act on that plan.[8]

As a man's soul is divided into three parts, so Plato's ideal society is correspondingly divided into three classes of people: the guardians, the warriors, and the money makers. The guardians are the lovers of learning and of wisdom—the philosophers. Corresponding to the part of reason in the individual soul, they are the only class that has freed its soul from its animal self and can ascend the heights, perceive the forms, learn from the forms, and apply what has been learned. For these reasons they are given absolute and totalitarian control over the just administration of the state.

The warriors correspond to the high-spirited part of the soul, which sides with reason when that soul is properly ordered and with the appetites when it is not. In the well-ordered state the warriors, fearless in their fight for the good and just, execute the guardians' designs with fervor and devotion.

The appetitive part of the individual soul is analogous to the lowest and largest class in the state. As the appetites represent the ''mass'' in the soul, so the money makers and the lovers of gain represent the masses in the state. To this class are delegated the artesans, the money lenders, and various other vocations concerned with worldly goods and pleasures.[9]

Order in a man's soul is necessary for him to live the best possible life; order in the state is necessary to insure the best life for the citizenry. The guardians (reason) are to rule; the warriors (thumos) are to fight for the rulers; the masses (appetites) are to be ruled. Each class is to perform the task befitting its nature and none other. Such social stratification— each part doing that which it does best—creates a conflict-free society, Plato argues; if each part pursues one line of activity, more than one value will not come into conflict. The guardians, as philosopher-kings, are the only class that has attained the highest cognitive state (intellection), which permits them to reach the forms and thereby to produce synthesizing explanations concerning the many forms. The guardians are, therefore, the only class which can be exposed to more than one line of activity. It is this ability to see the whole that allows the guardians to rule. The other two classes, being farther behind on the cognitive ladder, are to pursue just one thing, lest they be pulled from their places by conflicting information whose merits they are ill equipped to weigh.

Education

A large part of Plato's *Republic,* in which he outlines his ideal state in detail, is devoted to education. Education is, to him, the medium through which the different classes are trained to do what they do best and thus the medium through which the well-ordered state is maintained. Children are to be reared painstakingly from birth until the laws that order the state have been fully established within them.

All education takes place in an environment that Plato considers suitable for the development of philosopher-kings. Because the guardians are to be the philosopher-kings who possess absolute and totalitarian control over the administration of the state and because Plato believes that the quality of a thing presented is adopted by the person receiving, the environment surrounding the guardians from birth must contain only that which will promote their development:

> We must look for those craftsmen who . . . are capable of following the trail of beauty and grace, that our young men, dwelling . . . in a salubrious region, may receive benefit from all things about them, whence the influence that emanates from works of beauty may waft itself to eye or ear like a breeze that brings from wholesome places health, and so from earliest childhood insensible guide them to likenesses, to friendship, and to harmony with beautiful reason.[10]

Those who are to be the guardians are given a particularly difficult education lasting some fifty years. During this time their essential natures are subjected to continual rigorous testing and their reactions are observed closely. Those whose natures are strong enough to withstand the temptations of the lower and who either do not deviate from or who quickly return to the higher finally are established as philosopher-kings.

The guardians, as one would expect, receive an education that includes those things taught the two lower groups but encompasses far more. Indeed, the warriors and the guardians are to be taught, to a great extent, the same subjects. The difference between the curriculum for the two groups lies in the purpose for which the study is taught and not in the study itself. Both groups are to receive a blending of gymnastics and music—gymnastics to toughen and strengthen, music to soften and refine. This is to serve the high-spirited principle in the warriors and the love of knowledge in the guardians.

Both classes are to be versed in reckoning the number. The warriors must be knowledgeable of such things for purposes of war—the ordering of troops, the counting of ships, the plotting of strategy. The guardians must be knowedgeable of such things for the purpose of apprehending unity and the truth: if the individual is presented with contradictory perceptions (opposites), he requires a means of judging between them. This cognitive conflict leads the soul ruled by reason to seek through pure thought a synthesizing explanation (the forms). The study of pure numbers, conceivable only by pure thought, aids in the exercise of pure thought.

The guardians are to be taught geometry because it represents the knowledge of that which always is—the eternally existent; they are to be taught astronomy so that the heavens may be used as "patterns" to aid in the study of reality; they are to be taught harmony to aid in the investigation of the beautiful and the good. The warriors might use geometry in fashioning their weaponry, astronomy in plotting the course of their ships at sea, and harmony in inspiring their high-spirited natures to fight for the good.

The final and the highest study is the dialectic, reserved only for the guardians in whom reason rules. The dialectic is the mental exercise by which conceptions are critically analyzed and through which the individual comes to grasp first principles, or forms. Plato claims that it is the *only* method of inquiry that advances to the cause to find confirmation instead of relying on hypotheses that are confirmations of themselves.

Since what the money makers need to know and to be is considerably less than that of the higher two classes, they are free to pursue their roles earlier in life. Still, this group benefits, to some degree, from instruction. For example, money makers and lenders make use of the study of reckoning and number for the counting of money; artesans use geometry and number in construction; principles of harmony are applied to that which is constructed, so that the environment conducive to the development of the philosopher-kings can be maintained.[11]

Although the guardians have tasted the pleasure of gain (the main reward of the lowest class) and honor (the main reward of the middle class) from childhood, they alone have experienced the pleasure of wisdom. Through the application of wisdom to their experiences of gain and honor, they place these lower two pleasures in their proper places; they recognize that wisdom is the highest good. This insight is a prerequisite for those who are to rule.[12]

Justice

Justice is a major topic of discussion throughout Plato's dialogues. Although numerous passages are devoted to its definition, only two dialogues will be discussed here. These are Socrates's dialogue with Callicles in the *Gorgias* and with Thrasymachus in Book I of the *Republic*.

Gorgias was a renowned teacher of rhetoric during the time that Socrates was pursuing the dialectic. A teacher of rhetoric trains his students to speak well on any topic from both sides. The assumptions underlying this study are (1) there are no such things as absolute truths,

(2) right and wrong are determined by convention, and (3) the law is nothing more than human convention particular to a society. Callicles is both a pupil and a friend of Gorgias.

Callicles rejects conventional morality because it exalts temperance as a virtue, and temperance is antithetical to the hedonistic position of morality that Callicles accepts. Conventional morality calls law-abiding and nontyrannical behavior just. Callicles, however, argues that a rational man can have legitimate self-interested reasons for acting unjustly instead of justly (unjustly and justly according to convention), and that these self-interested reasons, for those who have the superior power to act upon them, take precedence over the rule of the majority (conventional morality). Following this stand, Callicles argues that in the highest state self-interest precludes what is conventionally called justice and, therefore, replaces it as the standard by which all else may be judged. Thus Callicles's hedonism, which advocates giving full reign to one's desires, becomes independent of other measures of value and itself determines judgments about the good and the evil.

Callicles separates natural law ("physei") from conventional law. He argues that what conventional law calls just—temperance and the subjugation of the appetites—is neither admirable nor beneficial because it restrains the superior man's natural right to his self-interested pursuits. These pursuits include indulging one's sensual appetites to their utmost so that one may be the more successful in fulfilling them.

Callicles argues that since the governing law of the animal kingdom is that the more powerful are to tyrannize the weaker, this should also be the governing law of man. The superior in physical form, mental acuity, and courageousness do and should prey upon and rule over the inferior in order to maintain the species. The inferior exist to serve and to maintain the superior. It is anathema to regress toward the mean, to equalize the extremes, because the diminishing of the superior for the sake of the inferior prevents progress. The superior have either been born into or have earned their superior rights, and it is just that they should have them. These rights include free access to all that the inferior man possesses, freedom to indulge one's sensual appetites without restraint, rule over the inferior, and power to determine the affairs of state.

Conventional morality is not natural justice, continues Callicles. Its laws were designed by the inferior and weaker and imposed upon the superior and stronger to prevent the superior from overreaching others at every turn.

In sum, common justice, according to Callicles, in restricting the reign of the superior man harms both the superior and the inferior—the superior because the opportunity to realize his great courage and intelligence is denied him; the inferior because he is deprived of the good things the superior man's wisdom and intelligence could bring him. The superior should not have to pay the price of conventional justice because natural justice (that the superior and stronger have the advantage over the inferior and weaker) precludes it.[13]

Socrates disagrees deeply with Callicles. He argues that the appetitive part of man is like a perforated jar that cannot be filled. Intemperant men who allow this part of their natures to rule chain their souls to the pursuit of things which can never be satisfied. Fools, they consume their lives in "sateless avidity," never knowing that something higher and better exists:

> I once heard one of our wise men say that we are now dead, and that our body is a tomb, and that that part of the soul in which dwell the desires is of a nature to be swayed and to shift to and fro. And so some clever fellow, a Sicilian perhaps or Italian, writing in allegory, by a slight perversion of language named this part of the soul a jar, because it can be swayed and easily persuaded, and the foolish he called the uninitiate, and that part of the soul in foolish people where the desires reside—the uncontrolled and nonretentive part—he likened to a leaky jar, because it can never be filled. And in opposition to you, Callicles, he shows that of those in Hades—the unseen world he means—these uninitiate must be the most unhappy, for they will carry water to pour into a perforated jar in a similarly perforated sieve. And by the sieve, my informant told me, he means the soul, and the soul of the foolish he compared to a sieve, because it is perforated and through lack of belief and forgetfulness unable to hold anything.[14]

To this Callicles answers that, once the jars are filled, there is no more pleasure in filling them, and the individual lives the "life of a stone." The pleasurable life requires the greatest possible influx.

What things are pleasurable? Socrates asks. Is it not necessary to distinguish between good and evil pleasures?

No, answers Callicles. The pleasant and the good are identical. If pleasure equals the good and if "evil" men (according to Socrates's definition) experience pleasure, then evil men must be good.

Pleasure, counters Socrates, is not identical with the good, for the good is an ultimate, single end (a form) and is a proper justification for the kind of life one lives; while pleasure is neither a single end nor is it suitable for justifying one's life. Pleasure is not responsive to the basic, deep intuitions we have about morality—especially justice.

Pleasure is not identical with the good because it is not possible to experience good and its opposite, evil, at the same time; while it is possible to experience pleasure and its opposite, pain, at the same time. For example, man is either in a state of bodily sickness (evil) or bodily health (good); he cannot be in both states or in neither state simultaneously but must possess and get rid of each in its turn. Good and evil are distinct. In contrast, it is possible to experience pleasure and pain at the same time. For example, thirst is to pain as drinking to satisfy the thirst is to pleasure. When a man drinks when thirsty, he is enjoying pleasure simultaneously with pain; when a man ceases at the same time from thirsting and from this pleasure in drinking, both pleasure and pain cease at the same time. Pleasure and pain are not distinct. Therefore, pleasure and the good are not identical.

Good is the higher because it is always good, while there are good and bad pleasures. Pleasure is to be had only for the sake of the good.

Goodness comes from harmony and order, not through the haphazard, but through the art that is assigned to each part. The ordered life represents a wholeness—a unity—and, in being so, is "satisfied with what at any time it possesses." Justice and temperance are the virtues which maintain that order.

The soul needs discipline and temperance, continues Socrates, to restrain it for its own good. For example, a man who has an illness of the body must discipline himself to eat the special foods that will cure it. Indulgence of the appetites would only further harm the very thing he seeks to cure. In like manner, the superior man has a rational plan for his life that requires not only courage and endurance (as Callicles claims) but also temperance; for, without temperance, the pursuit of the nonrational (appetitive) desires would necessarily restrict the rational ends. Thus, the temperate soul of the rational man is good while the intemperate soul of the irrational man is evil.[15]

Thrasymachus, in Book I of the *Republic,* offers an argument similar to Callicles's that the just is whatever is to the advantage of the stronger. Since the rulers are the stronger in a state, the just is that which is to their advantage. Thrasymachus further argues that since in daily affairs those whom Socrates would call "just" lose, while those whom Socrates would call "unjust" profit, it must be virtuous and wise to be unjust.

Socrates counters Thrasymachus's first argument by alluding to the arts as rulers of their art. An art exists, Socrates observes, not for its own advantage but for that which is ruled by it. The medical art, for example, as ruler and governor of the body exists not for itself, but for the advantage of the body it rules. In like manner, the rulers of the state rule not for their own advantage, but for the advantage of those whom they rule. Thrasymachus is mistaken in his argument that the just lose while the unjust gain, says Socrates. Injustice is disorder in the individual soul and city; it arises when a lower part interferes with the business of a higher. This *weakens* both the individual soul and city, for each part is then not doing that for which its nature is best adapted. Injustice in the individual soul renders one unable (because of inner conflict) to achieve anything, as injustice in a city renders the citizens incapable of effective action in common. The unjust soul and city have enslaved their best parts to their worst, and a wretched, evil condition it is to be enslaved to the most despicable and godless part; while the just soul and city have maintained the proper order within, and thereby live well. He who lives well possesses a blessed inner happiness that transcends all misfortune of external origin.

To do wrong, therefore, is worse than to suffer wrong, Socrates argues. The man who has done wrong has evil in his soul and is thereby in a most miserable condition; while the man who has been wronged, as long as he has not been robbed of his goodness, is unharmed. Just punishment will affect the soul and make it more just; just penalties cure a man of evil.[16]

Finally, Socrates claims that "to know the good is to do the good." Virtue (order and justice) is knowledge of the good; it is all man needs to live a happy life. This happiness is the final good toward which all mankind strives.

Kant

Like Plato, Kant separates man's world into two parts: the sensible, or phenomenal (material) and the intelligible, or noumenal (mind). Like Plato, he claims that first principles are a priori in that they are in the world of the intelligible where reason alone resides; they are outside of man's sensible world. Like Plato, Kant claims that the mind can grasp a priori moral principles because it works naturally in accordance with them. And, like Plato, Kant considers a priori principles to be the bases from which correct moral judgments are made.

This, however, is where agreement between these two philosophers ends. Kant argues that first principles come from the exercise of man's reason; reason provides the moral truths that are to guide man's actions. Plato insists that first principles are antecedently given with predetermined, fixed contents, and that they can be grasped by intuition alone. Man's rational nature is only the means of reaching the end of the forms. Reason is a vehicle by which the eternal truths are reached, but those truths are neither determined by nor embodied in reason.

In Plato's ideal society highly developed philosopher-kings are required to scale the heights, enter the intelligible region where the pure forms reside, learn from their truths, and apply what they have learned to the just administration of society. Although the journey is difficult and conceivable only for a few, entrance into the intelligible region is both possible and necessary. In contrast, Kant claims that man can never know the intelligible world (although he can conceive of it) because human knowledge is a combination of sense and conception which man ultimately cannot separate. Man must see himself as belonging to the intelligible world by nature of his intelligence, as he must also see himself as belonging to the sensible world by nature of his senses. Because he belongs to both, he is subject to the laws of both; but he can never leave the sense world behind totally and enter into the pure world of the intelligible. If man tries to separate these two parts of himself, says Kant, he runs the risk of losing himself in a world of shadows. To Kant, the intelligible world is an Idea—an Idea or an order different from that of the world of sense—but one which it is not possible to know.[17]

[These assertions raise questions to the thoughtful student of philosophy when they are examined in the light of Kant's association with Emanuel Swedenborg, the great scientist and seer who claimed he traveled some thirty years in the intelligible world while still living in the world of sense, and who wrote volumes detailing his purported experiences therein. Kant, at the request of a friend and because of his own deep interest in the occult, made close investigation of Swedenborg's powers and concluded that they were real: "What can be brought forth against the authenticity of these occurrences?"[18]

However, persistent efforts of Kant (who was then ambitious, middle class, impecunious, and unrecognized) to strike up a dialogue with Swedenborg elicited no response. In what can be described only as a vindictive reaction to Swedenborg's apparent snub of him, Kant developed a "sudden hatred for speculative metaphysics"[19] and eventually wrote, in a vitriolic attack on Swedenborg and metaphysics, *Dreams of a Spirit Seer*. Although Kant's revolt "manifested itself in a wanton destruction of everything that he once held sacred: the immortality of the soul, the ideal of a divine exemplar, the mystic union of the soul with the World Soul,"[20] his basic philosophical premises (the distinction between the noumenal and phenomenal worlds; the power of the spirit over matter) were assimilations of Swedenborg's writings.[21] In Part I of *Dreams of a Spirit Seer*, for example, Kant details his theory of spirits and calls Swedenborg's prior supporting empirical evidence mere coincidence.

It is also interesting to note that *Dreams of a Spirit Seer* (and, therefore, the evidence of Kant's tie to Swedenborg) was omitted from the *Kantstudien*—the official collection of Kant's works—and did not surface for one hundred years.[22]]

Both Plato and Kant agree that the mind can understand a priori principles because the mind works naturally in accordance with them. However, the reason the mind works naturally in accordance with them is a basis of disagreement. Plato argues that man's soul (as separate and immaterial) has at one time resided and will again reside in the region where the forms, or first principles, exist; man's affinity to their truths is based on his recollection of another, higher existence. Kant, on the other hand, claims that man's mind acts in accordance with first principles because they have come from man's pure practical reason.

Each of these two philosophers believes that there exists, either antecedently or by self-legislation, a supreme principle of morality. Plato calls it "the good" (an antecedent principle); Kant calls it the "categorical imperative" (a self-legislated principle). Plato rests on the assumption that once man knows the good he will act from it; there is no discrepancy between what one should do and what one does do, once one knows the good. Kant disagrees, observing that intervening, non-moral considerations such as immediate inclination and self-interest obscure ordinary man's desire to follow the moral law.[23] One can be sure he is doing a morally good act only if he acts from the motive of duty.

In sum, Plato encompasses the whole of mankind in his writings. Few people, in his view, are sufficiently developed to rule themselves; most require strict control by the more highly developed through the structure of the state. Not every man is born rational and every man's nature is not ipso facto moral; it *may* become so only after the most stringent upbringing and testing, which is to be provided by the state. In contrast, Kant focuses upon no man but the rational. He assumes that rational man has within himself from the beginning the ability to be a fully autonomous moral being and, thereby, to follow self-legislated moral imperatives without external interference. It is no business of the state or of anyone, argues Kant, to try to make men moral; "only the individual can do that for himself."[24] In consequence, the rights of the individual are paramount in Kant's theory; both morality and the laws are founded on those rights.

Kant's aim is to find the supreme, universal principle of morality which will justify all moral judgments. He first identifies what is good under all circumstances—that is, the highest good—and concludes that this is a "good will." A good will is good in itself; its aim is only to do good. It is manifested as a secure, good character that enables man to act from first principles. Such a character is moral in that it is determined by what a person means to do rather than what he manages to accomplish.[25]

One who acts from a good will cannot be blamed for ill results, for ill results do not detract from the moral value of an act done from a good will. A good will is not a natural gift, says Kant; natural gifts can be misused. Rather, natural gifts are "corrected" by a good will to serve universal ends.[26]

The moral value of an action depends on the unconditional moral value of the motive.[27] The motive of duty, argues Kant, is that which has unconditional moral value. Because duty is the only intrinsically admirable motive, a person having a good will acts for the sake of duty, and an action has moral value only when it is done for the sake of duty. A man may have a natural inclination to do the morally right thing, but natural inclination and talent may be led astray by other nonmoral considerations. For this reason, an act not done for the sake of duty may "deserve praise and encouragement," but it is not morally praiseworthy. It is only the individual who acts for the sake of duty who is worthy of moral esteem—and all the more so if the act has been done at the cost of a great moral struggle.[28]

The function of reason is to produce a good will. It is reason that controls action in man, decides moral judgments, and directs the natural gifts and gifts of fortune to serve universal ends. It is pure practical reason that formulates the moral laws ("objective maxims") in accordance with which man must act from the motive of duty. These laws have their genesis in and are justified by a supreme moral law which Kant calls the "categorical imperative." A categorical imperative is unconditioned and absolute (not based on a willing to further some end), universal (applicable to all rational beings), binding (upon all beings capable of thought and reasoning), necessary (necessitating that all rational beings act in a certain way), and morally good.[30] Its primary formulation is "Act only on that maxim through which you can at the same time will that it should become a universal law."[31] For example, suppose a person wishes to test the moral permissibility of the following maxim: "Whenever I believe myself short of money, I will borrow money and promise to pay it back, though I know I will never in fact repay it."[32] The person would have to ask himself how things would be if his maxim became a universal law. If it were to become a universal law, he would reason, promising would have no meaning, since no one would believe anything he was promised. The individual could not at the same time will that his maxim become a universal law and that he could promise anything with the expectation that he would be believed.

This primary categorical imperative has several alternative formulations: The Formula of the End in Itself ("Act so that you treat humanity, whether in your own person or that of another, always as an end and never as a means"), The Formula of Autonomy ("Act in harmony with the idea of the will of every rational being as making universal law"), The Formula of the Law of Nature ("Act as though the maxim of your action were by your will to become a universal law of nature"), The Formula of the Kingdom of the Ends ("Act as if you, by your maxims, were at all times a legislative member in the universal realm of ends").[33]

Central to the primary categorical imperative, its alternative formulations, and, indeed, Kant's theory of morals is the insistence that rational man is the endpoint of nature; that he exists for no purpose, or end, other than himself; and that he has, therefore, an ultimate and absolute value.

Rawls

Both Rawls and Kant maintain that moral laws are formulated by rational man. Kant argues that any moral principle is justified by its congruence with rational man's pure reason (having no part in man's anthropological self). Rawls, on the other hand, argues that any conception of justice is justified by its congruence with rational man's common sense (grounded in man's total social history). Rawls does not address an intelligible world separate from the sensible. Man's ordinary practical reason may legitimately claim to be true, says Rawls, and is, in fact, the basis for the formulation of first principles.[34] To Kant, the first subject of justice is the objective maxims of individuals in everyday life. To Rawls, it is the basic structure of society; its concern is with the fair distribution of basic rights and duties and with the fair adjudication of contending claims to the advantage of social life. Construction of the principles of social justice is achieved by unanimous collective agreement; individual decisions are then made in conformity with that collective agreement.[35]

Rawlsian theory is called Justice as Fairness. Its aim is through a specific procedure to explicate shared notions of common sense, which are implicit in the culture of a modern, democratic society and which form a foundation for consensus among rational moral people about allocation of resources and social privilege. Most importantly, Justice as Fairness aims to establish these shared notions as the foundation of its social institutions and as the standard by which the claims of all citizens are justly weighed.

The procedure for constructing first principles conforms to the tenets of "pure procedural justice." (This is to be distinguished from "perfect procedural justice" in which there is a predetermined standard to which the results must conform.) In pure procedural justice what is just is defined by the outcome of the procedure itself; there are no antecedent criteria. The primary requirement in Rawls's theory is that the deliberating agents share a general conception (1) of a well-ordered society (in which all citizens accept the first principles and the procedure for determining them, and in which the public institutions are in accordance with the first principles) and (2) of a free and equal moral person (a rational individual with a "workable" sense of justice who is entitled to influence the organization of his public institutions in order to advance his fundamental aims and "highest order interests").[36]

The first principles to be constructed must adhere to certain guidelines: They must be applied to all equally; they must effectively settle contending claims; they must be the highest standards from which to judge.[37] In addition, knowledge of them must be available to all.

The archetypal framework within which first principles are selected Rawls calls the "original position." The original position is a mediating model-conception which connects (1) the model-conception of modern man as a moral person and (2) the principles of justice which describe the relations between persons in the model-conception of a well-ordered society. The original position mediates between these two conceptions by modeling the way rational persons would ideally select first principles of justice for their society.[38] Additional characteristics that define the deliberating agents in the original position are as follows:

1. Each agent represents like persons. They are moral and have a common understanding of the good.
2. Each agent possesses two moral abilities: to understand and to act from principles of justice; and to create, to change, and to adhere to the shared idea of the good.
3. Each agent is rationally autonomous. He need not follow any antecedent principle of right and justice. He need be motivated only by a "higher order interest" in his moral powers and in advancing his moral ends.
4. Each agent understands that he functions in and represents a self-contained society in which all members are full participants, are in agreement in their conception of justice, and support their public institutions because those institutions reflect that conception.[39]

An additional constraint is placed upon the agents in the original position to insure fairness—the "veil of ignorance." Under this veil of ignorance, the constructing agents are made ignorant of their places in society, their inherent abilities, and their own ends.[40]

The actual procedure for constructing the first principles of social justice is fluid and complex; the reader is referred to Rawls's book, *A Theory of Justice,* for its particulars. In brief, the constructing agents must ideally role-take every position and contractual situation within the society, weigh each claim equally, and formulate a set of principles compatible with everyone's right to equal liberties.

Rawls is centrally concerned with the "deep" inequalities between people. These inequalities, according to him, are due primarily to "accidents" of social position and natural endowment. (He calls these gifts accidents because he believes that those who possess them have done nothing to deserve them.) Political institutions tend to reflect the biases of the more well-off and therefore to exacerbate the unequal situation that exists naturally. For this reason, principles of social justice must apply first to the inequalities that exist. From this conviction and from the procedure for establishing first principles of justice, Rawls concludes that there are only two fair principles of justice:

> First Principle: "Each person is to have an equal right to the most extensive system of equal liberties compatible with a similar system of liberty for all."
>
> Second Principle: "Social and economic inequalities are just only if they result in compensating benefits for everyone—the least advantaged in particular."[41]

Once the principles of justice are established, each person is free to pursue his individual good as he sees it, as long as he follows the ground rules. It is understood and accepted by Justice as Fairness that there will be great variations in religious, philosophical, and moral beliefs; and no effort is made to formulate universal standards in these areas.[42]

Rawls does require that the ideal well-ordered society honor what he calls the "most important primary good"—self-respect. Self-respect represents an individual's sense of his own value, his conviction that his life's plan is worth pursuing, and his confidence in his ability to carry out that plan.[43] Rawls rejects Plato's standard of perfectionism (rational intuitionism) because it passes judgment upon the relative value of a person's way of life.

Finally, the institutions in a well-ordered society are to shape the character and the aims of their members. Because of this critical role, the fundamental grounds of these institutions must be submitted to public scrutiny.

Kohlberg

Lawrence Kohlberg's theory of morality is a deontological, duties and rights, ethical theory (defining the moral "ought" as intrinsically valuable independent of any results obtained by acting upon it). In agreement with the theories of Kant and Rawls, Kohlberg claims that rational persons can harmoniously coexist through adhering to rational standards that they determine. This is not the rational intuitionism, or perfectionism, that Plato espoused. Kohlberg and Rawls in particular do not claim that first principles originate in antecedent causes, although they do not deny it. They state that antecedent causes are not necessary for objective knowledge of the material world.

Morality is a completely autonomous, formalistic domain to Kohlberg. It does not answer "Why be moral?" It does provide a *procedure* for arriving at a fair distribution of rights and of social advantage for the citizens of a modern, democratic society and a set of principles by which rational man is to make moral judgments.

Kohlberg's procedure, called "ideal role-taking," is drawn from Rawls's description of pure procedural justice within the original position. In any given situation ideal role-taking involves (1) imagining oneself in each person's position and considering all of the claims of each, (2) placing oneself under the "veil of ignorance" so that one does not know who he will be in the situation, (3) asking oneself if one could rationally uphold each person's claim, and (4) weighing the claims and acting in accordance with the highest.[44]

The set of principles is:

1. Respect for persons: "Treat each person as an end and never as a means."
2. Justice as equity: "Treat each man's claim impartially regardless of the man."[45]

Kohlberg agrees with Kant and Rawls that the principles of justice are ones that any rational member of a society would choose by virtue of his rationality.

Kohlberg's unique and laudable contribution to the study of morality has been his descriptions of how ordinary human beings actually reason about rights and duties. These descriptions have their basis in Piagetian cognitive theory, which holds that reasoning originates in and is developed by the interaction between the individual and his environment. That is, an individual assimilates (takes in) new material from his environment and accommodates (alters) himself in order to incorporate and to use the new material.

In his doctoral thesis Kohlberg postulated a universal, ontogenetic trend in the development of moral reasoning. To test this hypothesis he designed a series of moral dilemmas which elicited reasoning about issues of justice (see Appendix F). Longitudinal and cross-cultural research findings supported this postulation. The trend was described as "stages" of moral development; Kohlberg identified six, but fully developed only five. Further analysis found the stages matching several criteria of Piagetian cognitive theory: They were invariant and irreversible (all people progress forward through the stages in order; no stages are skipped; there is no backward movement), universal (stage sequence occurs ontogenetically; all persons move through them), and structured wholes (stages are comprehensive ways of thinking).[46] Higher stages represented more adequate ways of handling the subject matter because they were more in equilibrium and able to assimilate increasing amounts of data into a stable, structured whole. Each higher stage became more prescriptive and universal.

From his empirical research and from his study of philosophy and cognitive theory, Kohlberg concluded that the development of morality is not a process of learning arbitrary cultural rules and values. Instead, there appears to be an implicit moral structure within the individual which is "called out" through the interaction between man and his sociomoral environment. This interaction stimulates internal cognitive reorganization, which helps the organism attain a more equilibrated and inclusive level of understanding and reasoning.[47]

Kohlberg divides his five stages into three levels: the preconventional, the conventional, and the postconventional. Brief descriptions of the levels and more detailed descriptions of the stages follow. (The descriptions of Stages 1, 2, and 3 are drawn primarily from a manual on cooperation constructed by this author under the tutelage of Dr. Robert Selman, Harvard Graduate School of Education.)

Preconventional Level

At the preconventional level the individual follows group rules because he fears the physical or pragmatic consequences of breaking them. This level includes two stages.

Stage 1. The Stage–1 reasoner is essentially egocentric in his thinking and actions; events are viewed from his perspective only. He recognizes that another person is different from himself physically and may have a different interpretation of the same event than does he, but he is unable to coordinate that other viewpoint with his own. The inability to coordinate two or more perspectives (or roles) prevents the Stage–1 reasoner from participating in and from appreciating a reciprocally meaningful social system.

This egocentric focus, in addition, blinds the individual to the psychological states of others. Actions are evaluated solely from a physical perspective. The individual will rarely, if ever, refer to a person's psychological motivations for performing an act. Instead, he will focus upon the physical act and its physical consequences, as though the act and its consequences represented two halves of a closed circle: Wrong-doing is believed automatically to be followed by punishment (bad acts or persons will and should be followed by bad events); physical consequences determine the goodness or the badness of an act.

The Stage-1 reasoner is very fluid in his thinking and reactions; he is easily influenced by his environment. This fluidity typically is given shape, or controlled, by an authority who is viewed as omnipotent. It is the authority who sets limits and who defines what is right.

"Might makes right" to this thinker. The strong control the weak, and the weak should be obedient. Justice is defined not as equality or as reciprocity, but in terms of status, power, and possessions. (Interestingly, this is reminiscent of Callicles's argument with Socrates about the nature of virtue and of the just in the *Gorgias*.)

Stage 2. At Stage 2 the "other" is recognized as being a self-contained, separate individual who nevertheless has at his disposal the same repertoire of emotions, motivations, and behaviors as does every human being. This recognition of human continuity in individual difference is an important step towards social maturity for the Stage-2 reasoner. From this recognition comes the understanding that very different people may have the same reaction given an identical situation, and that behavioral differences within the same situation can be the result of differences in inner, psychological states. These psychological variables may or may not be discernable from without, but they can be understood by others because of their common human denominator. Thus intention, or motivation, is taken into account when the Stage-2 thinker interacts with or judges the actions of another. Also, punishment is no longer believed to follow wrong-doing automatically; one can hide his true intentions, and so can others.

Reciprocity at Stage 2 represents an instrumental exchange between two parties. Each party acts under the assumption that how he treats the other will determine to a great extent how the other will treat him. This involves the ability to stand outside of the self for a second-person perspective. It is rather simplistic and self-centered, however, because the motivations for prosocial acts are intrinsically self-serving ones: "If I do x for A, A will do x for me."

Fairness in the Stage-2 world represents a condition of equal exchange: each person has an equal right to an equal share of the goods. Authority is relative. All persons, including the authority, must abide by the rules. The principle of justice as liberty at this stage is expressed as each person's having a right to pursue his own interests and to expect noninterference from others. The belief is translated, however, outside of a conventional social system of affiliative and societal duties. At this stage there is little appreciation of the self's participation in a greater community to which one is bound by social obligation.

Finally, moral approval of an act is dependent upon a concrete projection of what the self would do in a similar situation. "Should" is indistinguishable from ''would'' at this stage, for both are seen to serve the self's instrumental interests.

Conventional Level

At the conventional level the individual follows group rules out of identification with and loyalty to the group. This level includes two stages.

Stage 3. Stage 3 rests upon the Stage–2 understanding of continuity in individual diversity. It adds the ability to ''reverse a reciprocal orientation'' (a Piagetian concept): the individual is aware that, as he tries to anticipate the other, the other also tries to anticipate him. This mutuality allows the Stage–3 reasoner to interact in a way more compatible with other people in his environment. (The Golden Rule, ''Do unto others as you would have them do unto you,'' is first understood correctly at Stage 3.) It also makes him very sensitive to how he appears to others. Understanding, forgiving, being viewed as a good person are central concerns at this stage.

The Stage–3 reasoner is able to imagine himself simultaneously in two roles, and from this, to arrive at a rationale for making a moral judgment. The limitation of this level of role-taking is that it is dyadic; the Stage–3 reasoner is able to coordinate no more than two claims at once. When asked if a husband should break the law and steal a drug from a druggist to save the life of his wife, the Stage–3 reasoner can imagine being in the positions of the husband, the wife, and the druggist and can coordinate any two of them; but he has difficulty assuming a third-party position simultaneously and deciding whose side the husband should take: should the husband consider the wife's claim first or the druggist's? (In situations like this one, the Stage–3 reasoner will most often place ties of close affiliation above other considerations.)[48]

Whether or not affiliation is a factor in the dilemma, the Stage–3 thinker uses stereotypes. Asked how a doctor should decide when confronted with the options of performing a mercy killing and violating the law that forbids that practice or adhering to the law and allowing his patient to die a painful death, the Stage–3 reasoner will use as justification for his moral judgment the stereotypical role of a ''good doctor.'' A good doctor may be one who cares for his patient by putting her out of her misery; or a good doctor may be one who honors the laws which, the Stage–3 reasoner believes, are established by benevolent lawmakers for everyone's welfare.

Perhaps the most unique social development at Stage–3 is the desire to conform to group expectations. Emphasis is placed on maintaining a social system in which moral concerns are intertwined with affiliative, social concerns. Justice requires the maintenance of good interpersonal relationships, which are based on stereotyped patterns of behavior. Negatively, there is as yet no framework within which strong differences of opinion can coexist without destroying the social balance; dissension is viewed as a threat to group cohesion. Those who do not fit the stereotypic roles adopted by a Stage–3 group cannot be accepted by that group if the group is to remain Stage 3, because what the disrupters are is not accounted for by that system.

Stage 4. Stage 4 is an advance over Stage 3 because it takes into consideration a more comprehensive and differentiated social unit. The Stage–3 group gives way to a more inclusive and a more impersonal collective social system which encompasses many affiliative units within its boundaries. The Stage–4 reasoner retains the ability to reverse a reciprocal orientation, but at this level the emphasis is on the relation between the individual and the social system.

Stage 4 is "law-maintaining."[49] Justice is a principle of social order, of laws agreed upon in a democratic society by the majority. This order exists to protect the well-being of the individual members of the society.

The collective system is maintained, in part, by a positive and negative reciprocity. That is, the beliefs that one should receive in proportion to what one gives, and that everyone owes something to the society in which he lives, are well-established rules of the Stage–4 social order.

Stage–4 reasoning is self-preservative in that there is no clear obligation to people outside of a particular society or to those who do not adopt the rules of that society and in that there are no rational guides for social change. Emphasis is only on maintaining the status quo.[50] It is limited in that it justifies the laws in terms of the institution but not in terms of a priori principles.

Postconventional Level

At the postconventional level the individual sees and lives by a priori moral principles, which societal laws are meant to reflect. This level includes one fully formulated stage.

Stage 5. At Stage 5 the law represents a social contract constructed by rational human beings, through mutual agreement, to protect everyone's basic human rights to life, liberty, and the pursuit of happiness. This "law-making" perspective is synonomous with Rawls's description of pure procedural justice in the original position, in which rules are constructed by rational lawmakers with the "proper orientation" (each is a member of a well-ordered society with shared notions of common sense; each sees himself as being a free and equal moral person) and with the rational consent of all of the members of that society. Stage–5 democracy is a procedural mechanism attractive to all rational members because its aim is to maximize the welfare of the individuals within the group and thereby to ensure representation for their self-interests.[51]

As described by Rawls's well-ordered society, the laws at Stage 5 represent the source from which conflicting group and individual interests around the social distribution of rights and the proper division of social advantages are resolved. As such, they are principles of social justice. Since these social principles are constructed by rational man, he is bound by them and their maintenance is of greater importance than the maintenance of any particular institution; at Stage 5 specific institutions are understood to embody the constructed social principles.

The limitations of Stage 5 become apparent when laws do not exist to cover a given situation or when the laws that do exist are questionable. There is no mechanism, for example, for incorporating the civil disobedience of a rational member of a well-ordered society at Stage 5. It is part of the contract between the citizen and the social order that the citizen obey the laws constructed by rational members for that order. This stage, in addition, maintains an arbitrariness about notions of the good and of moral, philosophical, and religious choice; it limits itself to the commonly based and shared beliefs about the social distribution of rights and the proper division of social advantages. Stage 5 fails, therefore, to provide substantive principles (or standards) of a universal morality to which all men should adhere.[52]

Moral Education

A significant portion of Lawrence Kohlberg's work has been dedicated to the practice of moral education. Kohlbergian moral education incorporates Plato's powerful tool for stimulating one's understanding of the just—the dialectic—in group discussions of controversial moral dilemmas. The aim is to create dissatisfaction with the person's present knowledge of the good so that he will expand and refine his understanding. Group moral discussion will often elicit more than one stage of moral reasoning. This is an important ingredient in producing moral stage growth. The higher stage reasoners create conflict in the minds of those lower stage reasoners with whom they argue; they thereby call out higher stage responses in their lower stage classmates. The teacher, as Socratic prober, clarifies the responses of the higher stage reasoners and then provides them with a dilemma which will elicit a still higher stage response.

The aim of education is to transmit the consensual values of society—the moral values in particular. Since justice (as liberty and equity) is the major moral value of democratic society, it is the proper content of moral education, says Kohlberg. The concern of moral education in a democratic society, then, is for the growth of justice in the child.[53]

The teaching of justice, Kohlberg argues, requires just schools. Just schools include all members in a democratic decision-making process where role-taking opportunities are available and responsible decision-making power is fostered. Students learn to weigh all points of view before making decisions that will affect the entire group. By this method a sense of the power, the seriousness, and the responsibility of the democratic process is instilled in them in a way not possible through passive instruction. *Active* participation in governance both stimulates moral reasoning and prepares the students to become more autonomous and just citizens who know how to work for the general welfare.[54]

This Author

This author is in philosophical agreement with Plato and in disagreement with Kant and Rawls. Kohlberg's explication of the stages of moral reasoning seem to her to reflect the reality that Plato addressed, although Kohlberg, himself, has claimed to be in sympathy with the philosophical underpinnings of Rawls in particular.

The fundamental differences between the philosophies of Plato and this author on the one hand and those of Kant, Rawls, and Kohlberg on the other lie in the stated endpoint of human development and the purpose of man's existence. To Kant, Rawls, and Kohlberg the endpoint of human development is the perfectly rational man; the perfectly rational man's purpose is to serve his own perfectly rational ends. There is no predetermined standard of the good (that man is capable of knowing, according to Kant; that is necessary for knowledge of the objective world, according to Rawls and Kohlberg) toward which man is to strive or by which his actions are to be guided. Rather, these philosophers assert that man's rationality (distinct from his anthropological self, according to Kant; embedded in his anthropological history, according to Rawls and Kohlberg) is sufficient to identify and to formulate the moral laws by which he is to live.

In direct opposition to these philosophies are the philosophy of Plato and that of this author: the endpoint of human development is not rational man, nor is man the source of the moral laws by which he is to live.

Rational man is one small part of an infinitely greater whole which is given life and meaning by the divine mind. All good within man comes from this source. To the extent that man directs his rationality to align himself with this divine within him is he involved in truth and goodness. To this extent that man regards *himself* as the cause and the endpoint of his being is he involved in falsity.[55] To the extent that man's social laws come into harmony with this divine mind does society ensure the conditions which allow man to evolve. Historical tradition and cultural intuition at their finest *reflect* the divine mind behind them; they are not, in and of themselves, the *origin* of truth.

Man's highest purpose on the physical plane is to align himself and his moral laws with the highest good that he is capable of receiving. His ultimate purpose is self-conscious reunification with the divine mind. (See point number 9 below.)

The specific points of this writer's philosophy follow.

1. Man belongs to a whole greater than himself, which encompasses, from exterior to interior,[56] at least four planes of existence: the physical, the astral, the mental, and the spiritual. The whole has its genesis in the divine mind—the infinite which contains within itself the cause of its continuation. From man's connection with this divinity stems the immortality of his soul.

2. The larger whole contains within itself an order. What man sees of nature—the seasons of the year, the waxing and waning of the moon, the movements of the planets in their orbits, the flood and ebb of the tides—follows an order. What man knows of the physical universe—from galaxies to subatomic particles—reveals an order. What man discovers in his physical universe reveals further order. Anomalies, such as the structure of Saturn's rings, impel a restructuring of scientific theory to include their realities; in other words, science's consciousness rises. Since the known shows order and the discovered indicates further order, it can reasonably be hypothesized that the to-be-known will continue to reveal order.

3. The evident order of the physical plane is informed by a not-so-evident order of the finer planes of existence—the astral, the mental, and the spiritual.[57] Each plane differs from the others in the refinement of the matter of which it is built and in the refinement of the vibrations required to act upon that matter. (For example, man's rationality is germaine to the physical plane only; the interior planes respond to the finer vibrations of intuition.) Each interior plane interpenetrates and thereby informs the one exterior to it.[58] (Rationality is, therefore, informed by intuition.) Between any two planes exists a nexus, which can be used by awakened souls to intuit information unavailable to the rational mind.

In any given spot a multitude of realities exist that correspond to levels of vibration, just as in any given area a multitude of radio stations simultaneously emit their special kinds of radio waves, each of which is received only by tuners set to the individual frequency on which that station operates. What an individual sees, experiences, or hears depends on the level or frequency to which he tunes.

4. Man has an individual order corresponding to that of the universe. His physical body is grounded in the material; his appetites and emotions (thumos) correspond to the astral; his mind corresponds to the mental; and his spirit corresponds to the spiritual.[59]

5. Man's purpose is to place himself in harmony with this universal order. To align himself harmoniously man must give priority, or rulership, to the highest (most interior) part of himself. The lower (more exterior) parts are in this way brought into the divine design by an ''inflow'' from above.

Those who fail to align themselves with universal order tend to experience life as chaotic and absurd. Examples of this can readily be found in the literature, music, and art of modern Western society.

6. As man places his individual parts in harmony with universal order, more power can be channeled through him: ''We are not to do, but to let do; not to work, but to be worked upon; and to this homage there is a consent of all thoughtful and just men in all ages and conditions. To this sentiment belong vast and sudden enlargements of power''— Emerson.[60] It is through placing themselves in harmony with this order of the universe that adepts such as Socrates have, through the ages, informed mankind:[61] ''Some thought him [Socrates] insane because he professed to have with him a spirit, or 'Dæmon,' as he called it, to whose voice he always listened.''[62] Men of genius, consciously or unconsciously, also draw their information from the higher, or more interior, planes. It does not come from *them* or from their rational faculties. Many have acknowledged this: ''Whenever I am confronted with a problem apparently impossible of solution, I seem suddenly to get the answer out of nowhere''—Thomas A. Edison.[63]

7. Disorder prevents the development of power. Randomly ordered molecules of iron, for example, have no magnetic power; but when the molecules in a piece of iron line up in orderly fashion, that is, north-south, north-south, that piece of iron becomes a magnet and has great power.

Man's highest potential cannot be realized when there is disorder within him—when he assigns rulership to his grosser parts, his appetites and emotions. If the grosser impulses are permitted to rule, they not only shut off the inflow from the finer planes, but can, in extreme cases, sever the man from his very source of being.[64]

8. Each man has his place and a particular work within the cosmic order. It is his responsibility to discover that place and to pursue the work that is his alone.

Throughout the ages men have sought by various means to ascertain their places within the cosmic order. Religious ritual has been a primary means. In many religions, however, inspiration turns to dogma, which stifles growth as it curtails individual questioning, ignores anomalies, and clings to fixated paradigms.

Philosophical systems are also attempts to place man within the universe. They, however, like religions, can be static and dogmatic. In addition, through misuse of erudition philosophy can lead man away from—instead of toward—the source of his being.

Such as Swedenborg, Joan of Arc, Luther, Socrates, Moses, Saul/Paul, and the Christ have found their places and their unique assignments through revelations from inner voices. This method, however, is not available to all. It requires people of spiritual elevation to contact the highest truths directly. Individuals of low spiritual development may be able to hear voices if they use the appropriate nexus, but they will contact only entities whose dominant vibratory rates correspond to their own. Great danger may result.[65]

Currently, the most accepted method by which man seeks to know where he stands in the universal scheme is science. Science must, however, exclude all that cannot be verified by the scientific method; it acknowledges only reason, whose application is limited to the physical plane. Thus, science would deny the validity of the voices of Swedenborg, Joan of Arc, Luther, Socrates, Moses, Saul/Paul, and the Christ.

One may then ask, "How *is* man to find his place and his work within the cosmic order?" Truest to this author's experience is the suggestion of John Spalding that this can be accomplished "first by endeavoring to live faithfully according to the truth [one] does see, and secondly by patient search for more truth."[66] It is this author's observation that if one perseveres on this path, he will be corrected and properly aligned with the universal order as the points of a compass are corrected when brought into precise adjustment with the lodestar.

9. Every part of the whole is in a cycle of orderly evolution. From unconscious unity with the divine mind, a monad is impelled to undertake a journey whose end is self-conscious reunion with the divine mind. En route, in conformity with the universal law of gender, this monad separates into male and female. First outward and downward, clothing itself in the matter of each plane through which it passes—spiritual, mental, astral, and finally physical—the evolving entity then begins the laborious journey back to its source, carrying with it full conscious knowledge gained from the experiences of each plane.[67]

These experiences lead the soul to the understanding that "the way to success lies in apprehending and giving actuality to the way of the universe, which, as a law running through end and beginning brings about all phenomena in time."[68] Some aspects of this law that can be known on the physical plane are the laws of mentalism, of cause and effect, of karma, of attraction, and of compensation.[69]

The law of mentalism states that an individual's external environment is a reflection of his inner mental state: nothing comes to a person which he has not summoned. Therefore, each of us is fully responsible for his life situation. It is through accepting this responsibility that the individual learns to change his creative thoughts and, eventually, to change his external reality. When one blames his problems on external sources and thereby separates himself from a situation he has created, he is prevented from taking hold of and changing that part of himself which causes his difficulty. He becomes an ineffective malcontent who cannot evolve because he is separated from his source of change and is dependent upon those things which, in themselves, have no power to effect change.

The laws of cause and effect, of karma, and of attraction inform this truth: every effect has a cause. To focus only on the effect without understanding its genesis renders all attempts to alter the effect ultimately useless. The law of karma (known in the physical realm as Newton's third law of motion) states, "For every action there is an equal and opposite reaction." By the law of attraction, what one is within will attract like people, circumstances, and environments without.

The law of compensation states that development occurs only through the individual's own efforts. If one makes no effort, he makes no real gain. It is an impossibility to confer from without that which must be built from within.

10. Judgment is *required* for evolution. Because there is an objective standard of the good, man can judge acts according to the degree of their adherence to this standard. Because man is not himself the end but is involved in a process of perfection, protecting his right to self-respect when that self-respect is grounded in falsity defeats the purpose for which man exists: to reunite with the divine mind.

Every man is on the path of evolution but, naturally, not all men have traveled the same distance. For this reason the claims of the man farther along the path deserve greater consideration. He has a higher, clearer, and more-encompassing view of the truth and is better equipped to work for universal welfare. Kohlberg's developmental stages of moral reasoning support this.

Notes

1. John Rawls, "Kantian Constructivism in Moral Theory," *The Journal of Philosophy,* vol. 77, no. 9 (September 1980): 557–564.

2. Plato, *Phaedo*, trans. Hugh Tredennick (Harmondsworth, England: Penguin Books 1954); reprinted in *The Collected Dialogues of Plato*, eds. Edith Hamilton and Huntington Cairns, Bollingen Series LXXI (Princeton: Princeton University Press, 1961), pp. 53–89.

3. Ibid., p. 57.

4. Plato, *Republic*, trans. Paul Shorey (Cambridge: Harvard University Press, 1930, 1935); reprinted in *The Collected Dialogues of Plato*, eds. Edith Hamilton and Huntington Cairns, Bollingen Series LXXI (Princeton: Princeton University Press, 1961), pp. 743–747.

5. Ibid., pp. 747–749.

6. Ibid., pp. 807–809.

7. Ibid., pp. 813–814, lines 586a–b.

8. Ibid., p. 814.

9. Ibid., pp. 667–688.

10. Ibid., p. 646, lines 401b–d.

11. Ibid., pp. 630–661.

12. Ibid., p. 772.

13. Plato, *Gorgias*, trans. W.D. Woodhead (New York: Thomas Nelson and Sons, 1953); reprinted in *The Collected Dialogues of Plato*, eds. Edith Hamilton and Huntington Cairns, Bollingen Series LXXI (Princeton: Princeton University Press, 1961), pp. 265–274.

14. Ibid., p. 275, lines 493a–c.

15. Ibid., pp. 275–289.

16. Plato, *Republic*, pp. 586–605.

17. Immanuel Kant, *Groundwork of the Metaphysics of Morals*, trans. and analysed H.J. Paton (New York: Harper and Row, 1964), pp. 118–121.

18. Mrs. St. Clair Stobart, *Torchbearers of Spiritualism* (Port Washington, N.Y.: Kennikat Press, 1925), p. 195.

19. John Manolesco, Introduction to *Dreams of a Spirit Seer*, by Immanuel Kant (New York: Vantage Press, 1969), p. 14.

20. Ibid.

21. Ibid., pp. 17–19.

22. Ibid., p. 22.

23. Kant, *Groundwork*, p. 61.

24. John Ladd, Introduction to *The Metaphysical Elements of Justice* (Indianapolis: The Bobbs-Merrill Company, Inc., 1965), pp. ix–xi.

25. Kant, *Groundwork*, p. 62.

26. Ibid.

27. Bruce Anne, *Kant's Theory of Morals* (Princeton: Princeton University Press, 1979), pp. 9–11.

28. Kant, *Groundwork*, pp. 65–67.

29. Ibid., p. 64.

30. Anne, *Kant's Theory*, pp. 36–37.

31. Kant, *Groundwork*, p. 88.

32. Anne, *Kant's Theory,* p. 53.

33. Kant, *Groundwork,* pp. 95–102.

34. Rawls, *Constructivism,* p. 519.

35. Ibid., p. 517.

36. Ibid., pp. 520–523.

37. John Rawls, *A Theory of Justice* (Cambridge: The Belknap Press of Harvard University Press, 1971), p. 11.

38. Rawls, Constructivism, p. 520.

39. Ibid., pp. 525–528.

40. Rawls, *Justice,* pp. 136–142.

41. Ibid., p. 302.

42. Ibid., pp. 447–448.

43. Ibid., p. 440.

44. Lawrence Kohlberg, "The Claim to Moral Adequacy of a Higher Stage of Moral Judgment," *Journal of Philosophy,* vol. 70, no. 18 (1973): 644–645.

45. Lawrence Kohlberg, "From Is to Ought: How to Commit the Naturalistic Fallacy and Get Away with it in the Study of Moral Development," *Cognitive Development and Epistemology,* ed. T. Mischel (New York: Academic Press, Inc., 1971): 212.

46. Ibid., pp. 167–171.

47. Ibid., p. 183.

48. Ibid., p. 198.

49. Ibid., p. 199.

50. Ibid., p. 200.

51. Ibid., p. 202.

52. Ibid., pp. 204–205.

53. Lawrence Kohlberg, "Education for Justice: A Modern Statement of the Platonic View," in *Moral Education,* eds. Nancy F. and Theodore Sizer (Cambridge: Harvard University Press, 1970).

54. Ibid.

55. Emanuel Swedenborg, *Heaven and Hell,* trans. George F. Dole, 2nd ed. (New York: Swedenborg Foundation, Inc., 1979).

56. Ibid., passim.

57. Annie Basant, *The Seven Principles of Man* (Wheaton, Illinois: The Theosophical Publishing House, 1972), p. 101.

58. Swedenborg, *Heaven and Hell,* passim.

59. Basant, *Seven Principles.*

60. Ralph Waldo Emerson, "Worship," in *The Works of Ralph Waldo Emerson (In One Volume)* (New York: Black's Readers Service Company, no copyright date), p. 383.

61. C.W. Leadbeater, *The Astral Plane* (Wheaton, Illinois: The Theosophical Publishing House, 1977), p. 5. Also in C.C. Zain, *Personal Alchemy* (Los Angeles: The Church of Light, 1949), p. 86.

62. William C. Morey and Irving N. Countryman, *Countryman's*

Edition of Morey's Ancient Peoples (U.S.A.: American Book Company, 1933), p. 216.

63. Dal Lee, *Understanding the Occult* (New York: Paperback Library, 1969), p. 109.

64. Besant, *Seven Principles,* pp. 54–55.

65. Zain, *Personal Alchemy* (Los Angeles: The Church of Light, 1949), pp. 30–31.

66. John Howard Spalding, *Introduction to Swedenborg's Religious Thought* (New York: Swedenborg Publishing Association, 1956), p. 234.

67. C.C. Zain, *Astrological Signatures* (Los Angeles: The Church of Light, 1952), pp. 115–119.

68. Richard Wilhelm and Cary Baynes, trans., *The I Ching,* with Forewords by Carl G. Jung and Hellmut Wilhelm, Bollingen Series XIX, 3rd ed. (Princeton: Princeton University Press, 1977), p. 5.

69. Three Initiates, *The Kybalion: Hermetic Philosophy* (Chicago: The Yogi Publication Society, 1940).

2 Descriptions

The Application of Theory to Reality

During the 1978–1979 academic year, this author (as teacher and sole researcher) applied Kohlbergian moral education, her own philosophy, and a behavior-modification system to a class of severely disturbed early adolescents.

Kohlbergian Moral Education

Democratically run class meetings were held every Friday afternoon. In these meetings classroom issues were discussed and proposed resolutions were voted upon. At first the teacher chaired the meetings; later students chaired them on a rotating basis. Each person—student and teacher—had one vote.

Moral-dilemma discussions with Socratic probing were occasionally held on Thursday afternoons. The degree of teacher direction at these times was dictated by the pupils' exhibited collective ability to direct themselves. Rules of behavior enforced from the beginning were (1) raise your hand when you have something to say, (2) let the person who is talking finish, (3) answer each other civilly and verbally, and (4) stay seated.

A major component of moral reasoning is the ability to role-take: to see another's point of view and situation. In order to do this, one must be able to appreciate individual diversity within human continuity. This is something that disturbed children are often unable to do. They experience difficulty in establishing personal boundaries and, therefore, in separating themselves from the stimuli (including fellow students) around them. Because they are unable to get a grasp of themselves, they do not fully recognize the individuality of others. One way to foster role-taking ability is to set aside a particular time during the day in which individual students can talk about themselves—their lives outside of the classroom and their personal concerns. This gives the students an opportunity to hear daily about lives which are different from, yet similar to, their own. It is hoped that they will, from this activity, come to identify specific points of differences and similarities.

To this end this teacher introduced "Sharing Time," which was held at the beginning of every school day (until it was discontinued in the spring for reasons which will be subsequently discussed). This activity afforded each child the opportunity to share his out-of-school experiences with the class.

This Author's Philosophy

This teacher's aim was to create a classroom atmosphere which vibrated at a level higher than the students' own in order to affect them—at first unconsciously and later consciously. The room was kept bright, neat, cheerful. The bulletin board had either a quotation that spoke to the spiritual laws directly or a lovely poem to stimulate the finer affections. Low-vibratory behaviors were not reinforced. For example, graffitti was erased without comment the day it was written. When the content of Sharing Time began to vibrate at a level markedly lower than that of the classroom environment, Sharing Time was eliminated; in its place the class copied, read, memorized, and discussed the meaning of famous quotations and poems that reflected upon high and positive ways to approach life. (See Appendix D for the quotations.) Most important, a daily story time exposed the students only to books that emphasized a transcendent being, eternal values, and/or objective standards of right and wrong. Prominent among these were the seven books of the *Chronicles of Narnia* by C.S. Lewis and *The First Jungle Book* by Rudyard Kipling.

Behavior Management

A simple behavior-modification system encouraged self-control. The results of a student's actions were immediately reflected in an external and impartial measure. The system consisted of points which positively rewarded or punished behaviors. A student earned points by engaging in school-appropriate behaviors such as attending to schoolwork, participating in group lessons, raising his hand, working quietly, following teacher directions, stopping and starting work on time, acting appropriately at the lunch table, standing in line correctly, and speaking civilly. He lost points by engaging in behaviors not appropriate in a school setting, such as failing to start or to stop work on time, not raising his hand, refusing to follow teacher directions, harassing other students, cursing, fighting, teasing, running in the hallways, sliding down the bannister, not attending to the lesson, and wasting time.

The point system was plotted in multiples of five. A student could earn a total of 200 points a day for engaging in appropriate student behaviors. He received 100 points upon his entry into the classroom and he could earn the remaining 100 during the day. The day was roughly divided into thirty-three-minute blocks, each block representing 10 points; at the end of a block a student received 10 points if he had engaged in appropriate student behaviors.

The negative behaviors were assigned different point values depending upon the seriousness of the behavior. Fighting, harassing, and not following directions, for example, had the highest negative point value (25 points); while not raising the hand and wasting time had the lowest (5 points). Whenever a student engaged in one of these behaviors he lost the corresponding number of points. For example, in one thirty-three-minute block a student could earn ten points for acting appropriately in general and lose five points for not raising his hand during a class lesson.

At the beginning of the year and whenever disturbed behaviors were at their strongest, this teacher stopped every thirty-three minutes to award points. After the classroom behavioral standards had been established or reestablished as the norm, this frequent awarding of points became unnecessary; points were then awarded after longer intervals two or three times a day. Negative behaviors, however, elicited an immediate loss of points throughout the school year.

A reward system accompanied the earning of points. A student had to earn a certain number of points in order to participate in lunch recess, end-of-the-day recess, and the end-of-the-week treat (a walk to a local store and fifty cents from the teacher or a hike through a favorite walking area).

In March a bonus-point system was instituted for the recitation of carefully chosen quotations and poems, for reasons that will be further explained in the winter anecdotal records.

A point chart with a movable pointer by each student's name was displayed in front of the room as an external measure of behavior. Next to this was a chart on which each student's accumulated points were recorded daily. On Friday each student totalled his own points for the week to determine his eligibility for the end-of-the-week treat. (See Appendix E for sample behavior-modification chart.)

The School and the Students

The experimental class was housed in a public school for emotionally disturbed and learning-disabled elementary and junior-high-aged children. This school, hereafter referred to as Valley Brook, served several school districts and accommodated approximately 125 students, sixteen teachers, and sixteen aides—with two adults and an average of eight students per classroom. It had its own principal, academic supervisor, social worker, crisis teacher, and part-time consulting psychiatrist.

The principal had worked with special-needs children for forty years and was respected for her knowledge and expertise. Her onerous responsibilities included closely screening all prospective students and their parents, interviewing and hiring all teachers, composing classes according to type and severity of disturbance and/or learning disability, matching teachers to classes, dealing daily with volatile students who could no longer be contained in their classrooms, calming teachers, and attending to routine administrative duties. She had been pressured by her superiors to remain for the 1978–1979 academic year despite her strong desire and definite plans to retire at that time.

This particular year was unusually difficult: our previous building had been declared unfit for elementary-school occupancy, and we were to move into a public elementary school in another town which had extra classrooms due to declining enrollment. We were leaving a beautiful setting where we had enjoyed acres of wooded land; a stream with a waterfall; an old and interesting school building in an exquisite, upper class town; and almost total autonomy. We were moving into a typical, 1950s-built elementary school next to a cemetery in a lower middle-class neighborhood as "guests."

In the new location most of the academic materials were in boxes and by principal's edict remained unavailable for many weeks. This caused severe limitations for all classrooms, particularly the most disturbed. Children need daily direction and structure; because their internal controls are lacking, emotionally disturbed children especially so. Structure in a school situation depends heavily upon the academic materials.

This author and her class were facing a more-serious academic situation than most of the other classes. Her students were the oldest and the most disturbed and several would soon require instruction beyond the materials available. Obtaining higher level academic materials was, therefore, a major concern of this teacher. She addressed the subject in the first teachers' meeting. Reaction from the principal was unexpected and unbending: any available money would be spent on materials for lower grades; none would be allotted for upper levels; no attempt would be made to secure appropriate materials. This teacher was advised to use library books for reading instruction.

This suggestion was a poor one. First, library books are not suitable for daily reading instruction; they supplement it. Differences between supplementary and instructional reading material are immediately obvious—the former are not geared to honing specific skills and have no developmental sequence. Second, the library had few upper level materials.

It became clear to this researcher that she would have to secure most of her own materials. This she was able to do through personal contacts in another school district. Fortunately, the materials were dated and, for this reason, excellent; they covered skills more in depth and required far greater mental concentration than do the newer academic materials.

Description of the Students

The students comprising the experimental classroom were unusually disturbed. They had been grouped together because of their comparatively advanced ages (seven were thirteen years old, two were twelve) and the severity of their socioemotional difficulties. A highly experienced male applicant had been courted for this particular class, and his last-minute decision not to accept the job left the principal without a teacher who she felt was strong enough to handle the group.

This author had just returned to the school after a year's leave of absence at the Harvard Graduate School of Education where she had studied Kohlbergian moral education. She was anxious to apply Kohlbergian techniques to disturbed children (their potential application to this population was what had originally attracted her), but was most reluctant to take a class of severely disturbed children for fear that the extent of their disturbance would occult any benefit to be derived from Kohlbergian techniques. Particularly disturbed children are often severely deficient in rational decision-making ability—the essence of Kohlberg's theory. This teacher was, therefore, most distressed when the principal assigned the above-mentioned group of students to her with the comment, "Try to morally develop these."

The year began with nine pupils and two adults (one teacher and one aide). Within the first six weeks, two of the students had changed residences and school districts. The remaining seven had low-average to average intelligence, were from low-middle and middle socioeconomic backgrounds, and suffered multiple home problems. Six were male, one was female; five were Caucasian, two were black. One had come directly from his district school and six were incorrigibles from the previous year's classes at this county school. Three of the seven had been resident patients in a local state mental hospital and were still considered seriously disturbed. A fourth had spent five of the previous six years at an institute for the retarded and severely learning disabled. A fifth, an antisocial incorrigible, had spent the previous two years in a home for children with minimum contact with his mother and siblings. The sixth and seventh also had serious problems of social attitude and adjustment. A more-detailed description of these seven students is given in the following paragraphs.

John, thirteen years old, had one of the most traumatic early childhoods of any of the children in the experimental class. Extremely serious home problems necessitated John's being placed with his grandparents until he was five and a half years of age. It was reported to this researcher that during those years he was physically undernourished and that he developed seizures.

The mother reported to this researcher that John had had difficulties in school from first grade. At eight he was referred for testing and found to be functioning in the educable mentally retarded range. During the next school year (his fourth) John was placed in an educable mentally retarded class. There he was reported to have been hyperactive and partially uncontrollable. (At some time John was placed on the antihyperactive drug Ritalin, which was discontinued when he was ten.) By the end of this year, the teacher felt John had improved enough to be retested and considered for another placement. It is unclear to this researcher what action was taken, but she suspects that John was returned to regular-class placement.

John's tenth chronological (fifth school) year brought to a head behavioral difficulties both at home and at school. He was hyperactive, impulsive, attention seeking, explosive, incessantly talking, stealing, enuretic, and dependent upon adults to help him fight his self-made battles. At school, in addition to the above, he had difficulty relating to his peers, an insistent attitude about being right even when he was wrong, and a tendency to wander around and to chatter to anyone he saw.

In August, the beginning of John's eleventh chronological year, he was admitted as an in-patient to a local state mental hospital. He remained there for the entire school year.

In September of John's twelfth year, he entered Valley Brook School. This researcher has virtually no information on his progress during that year. She does know, however, that his classroom teacher suffered repeated bouts of a serious illness and was absent much of the year. As a result, the class had a series of substitute teachers and was often in upheaval.

Twelve-year-old Matthew had had trouble with school since first grade, which he repeated because of hyperactivity, clownishness, and a short attention span. By third grade he was considered a loner and hostile towards his classmates.

Matthew's mother reported that he was also hostile towards his four siblings and other children. When corrected, he would say that no one loved him and that he felt like killing himself. He set fire to an abandoned house in the neighborhood.

At this time Matthew was given a battery of diagnostic tests. His intelligence test was 21 points higher than it had been three years earlier (from average to superior). Overall functioning was questionable, however, because of the unevenness of his various subtest scores, which ranged from dull normal (number skills) to the very superior levels (abstract thinking, general information, and details). The psychiatric diagnosis was latent schizophrenia with organic features: Matthew was labeled insecure, cautious, suspicious, immature, regressively aggressive, and as exhibiting little automatic self-control. The recommendation was that he be institutionalized.

Matthew's tenth chronological (fourth school) year was spent as an in-patient in the local state mental hospital. Verbal reports from John and Nicole, another student in this author's classroom, (who were both in-patients while Matthew was) and from reliable adults describe him as having been a very disturbed, insecure child who was totally unwilling to face his problems. The staff considered him to be one of the most difficult patients and, in fact, described him as "their worst." Matthew was released from the hospital with reservations, the staff feeling that little had been accomplished.

In September of Matthew's eleventh chronological year he entered Valley Brook School. His teacher spoke of her year with him with deep frustration. He could not relate to his peers; he was impulsive; he was totally incapable of participating in classroom activities and had to be isolated from the group for most of the year; he appeared to live in a private world which he did not share. The year ended with Matthew's teacher feeling that her efforts with him had been unsuccessful.

Thirteen-year-old Andrew had an early history of language difficulty. His mother told this researcher that he had developed normally until he was two and a half. At that time he contracted pneumonia and ran a high fever. From then on, she said, Andrew exhibited significant delays in speech development.

Andrew began his school career as a day student at an institute for severely learning-disabled and mentally retarded children; he was considered mentally retarded. At the end of five years his intelligence test score had risen to the normal range, and his diagnosis had changed from retarded to learning disabled. This change in status prompted Andrew's parents to insist on immediate regular-class placement and Andrew was placed directly into a regular fifth-grade classroom. There he exhibited serious problems, both academically (barely reading at the second-grade level) and behaviorally (demonstrating a limited understanding of cause and effect and engaging in aggressive behaviors towards his peers).

That spring Andrew was referred for testing for alternative placement. Individual interviewing revealed a boy who was quite concerned about his learning problems and school placement and who was excessively self-critical and depressed. Andrew was referred to Valley Brook School.

Andrew's first year at Valley Brook was successful. He was placed with a conscientious teacher who became extremely involved with him personally. Here Andrew made significant progress academically and behaviorally, although he still would lapse into violent outbursts when frustrated and remained aloof from his peers. He also talked very little.

Twelve-year-old Thomas was the youngest of nine children in a low-income, inner city family. By the time he was born, seven of the other eight children had been removed and sent into foster placement and his father had died. When Thomas was six he found out that he had other siblings. (Some of them began to visit the home.) Two of them moved in, taking his room; the oldest sister, on whom he had depended, moved out. For the next three years Thomas repeatedly ran away from home and from school. He was finally removed from his home and placed in first one and then another shelter.

During Thomas's eleventh chronological year he was placed by the Department of Public Welfare in a long-term home for children, with no plans for his return to his mother. In September he entered Valley Brook School. His teacher (the same one to whom John was assigned) suffered repeated bouts of a serious illness and was absent much of the time. The class was run by a series of substitutes and was in continual upheaval. Thomas was reported to have been a serious behavior problem and quite difficult to control. A dual personality was in evidence here: he would swing from being violent and angry to being pleasant and personable.

Thirteen-year-old Philip had a long history of school difficulties. He had to repeat one grade and was reported to have had a violent temper which manifested itself in frequent physical confrontations with his classmates and in a defiant attitude towards adults (several of whom he provoked into striking him). Philip demanded a tremendous amount of individual attention. For example, he would pay no attention while a group lesson was being explained and then demand a personal explanation when it was time to do the lesson. If the teacher ignored him, he would create a disturbance. She would then have to spend an inordinate amount of time reasoning with him about his attitude or he would sulk and refuse to do anything at all.

At home Philip was having temper tantrums, and his parents (who were unwilling to strike him) were frustrated at his lack of success in controlling his violent behavior. Despite this, they refused to permit the psychiatric evaluation requested by his principal and his teacher.

At twelve years of age, Philip entered Valley Brook School. Placed in the previously mentioned class in chaos because of the teacher's illness and absences, he was reassigned in the middle of the year, entering a class full of street-wise, acting-out, early adolescents. Here the teacher ran a loosely structured program in which the students were expected to set their own limits. She commented on Philip's extreme and constant anger.

Thirteen-year-old Peter had had problems in school and at home from kindergarten on. At home he was nasty towards his peers in the neighborhood and played successfully with only younger children. In school he was unable to establish a positive relationship with anyone but his third-grade teacher; he stole; he was a physical and verbal annoyance to the other children; he was perceived as being completely unmotivated to modify his behavior; he was summarily rejected by his classmates; he had an extremely negative self-image. Perhaps one of the causes of Peter's negative self-image was a sexual confusion. His mother complained of his effeminate behavior. In fourth grade Peter was placed in a special class for the emotionally disturbed, where his behavior visibly improved.

In November of Peter's sixth school (twelfth chronological) year, his family moved for the second time. As his new school was not informed of his previous special-class placement, Peter was placed in a regular sixth-grade classroom. Immediately, his teacher noticed severe social and emotional problems: he entered into verbal battles with his peers, engaged in socially inappropriate behaviors, came to school physically disheveled, and formed symbiotic attachments to any authority figure who showed him care. In addition, he consistently denied his role in the creation of his problems at school. He maintained that all fights were started by the other students.

Psychological testing revealed Peter had a sensitivity to interpersonal nuances but a disregard for social conventionality and intense mental confusion (performing at a level six years behind his chronological age on the Bender Gestalt).

In September of 1978, Peter entered this author's class at Valley Brook School.

Thirteen-year-old Nicole, the only girl in the class and the only girl in a family of four children, had had trouble in school since second grade. Loud and complaining, dashing about the classrooms, hallways, stairways, and playground, unable to focus on learning activities, in the spring of her third school year Nicole was place on the antihyperactive drug Ritalin (which she took for the next three years). In November of her fourth school year, both she and her brother (one year older) were placed by their parents in a children's home, where they remained until June. In September (her sixth school year) Nicole was placed in a special education class in her district school. In January she was removed from there and placed in a tutoring program for which she had to be present in school only one and one-half hours a day.

By April she had to be removed from the school system altogether and was admitted to a local state mental hospital as an in-patient. Nicole was released from the hospital during the summer before her seventh school year and returned to her family.

In September twelve-year-old Nicole was placed in Valley Brook School. This author has little information on Nicole's first year at Valley Brook. Nicole herself recalled her behavior during that year in an essay: "Last year I was fairly well, but sometimes I would make fun of Carrie and I would sometimes fight with James and I would slam people's classroom doors and I would run around the school and a lot of times I would be in the principal's office and my parents would have to come and talk to her and they would be very angry and I usually got into a lot of trouble—from my mom and dad—and I was not allowed out.''

These seven students were joined by six other students for varying lengths of time throughout the school year. Keith and Carrie entered the class in the beginning of the year and moved from the district in late October. Wayne entered in December and left in January. David and Charles entered in February and March, respectively, and remained until the end of the school year. Lloyd was with the group for only the final two weeks. Although these six students' (especially David's) contributions to the classroom atmosphere are included in the narrative (chapter 3), they are not considered part of the core experimental group.

3   Narrative Analysis

This chapter contains a clinical, developmental, narrative analysis of the growth of community within the class composed of the previously described seven students. The democratically run class meetings were tape-recorded and transcribed. In addition, this teacher kept daily anecdotal records.

Behavioral descriptions from the anecdotal records have been conjoined with the reasoning of the students during the class meetings to provide the content for the analysis of the growth of community. Specific emphasis is placed on (a) initial group reasoning and behavior, (b) internal and external crises which significantly affected the group, (c) group resolutions and attempts to integrate the crises, and (d) the resultant changes in group behavior, reasoning, and attitudes.

The dominant lines of reasoning exhibited by the students during the class meetings and, where applicable, the behaviors described in the anecdotal records, have been scored for stage of sociomoral reasoning. This has been done to illustrate the process of the group's moral-stage progression from September to June. In addition, the community meetings have been analyzed for (a) phase and stage of collective normative values and (b) stage of the sense of community valuing. Collective normative values are group values reflected in rules and general group policies (for example, not stealing, eat with manners). A norm phase describes the extent to which the normative value is accepted by the community. There are seven phases:

Phase	Description[1]
0	No norm is proposed.
1	Individual proposes norm.
2	Norm is accepted.
3	Members expect the norm to be upheld.
4	Expectations are disappointed.
5	Community expresses disapproval.
6	a) Individual(s) report violations anonymously.
	b) Individual(s) report violations publicly.

The sense of community valuing is self-explanatory.

The stages of collective normative values and the sense of community valuing are determined by morally staging the most frequent student statements concerning both. For example, Stage 2 is grounded in concrete rights and needs and in instrumental exchange ("tit for tat"). As previously outlined in the discussion of Kohlberg's Stage 2, there is little appreciation of the self's participation in a greater community to which one is bound by social obligation. Stage 3, the age-appropriate goal for a class of early adolescents, is grounded in a group conformity in which moral concerns are intertwined with affiliative social concerns. Emphasis is on caring for the group (which is often viewed as familial), on sharing, and on being a good group member. As previously outlined, those who do not fit the stereotypic roles adopted by a Stage–3 group cannot be included.[2]

Throughout the year this author's philosophy informed the vast majority of her teaching policies and decisions. Flowing like an underground river, it surfaced during daily story time, whenever major problems were discussed, and whenever specific actions or events most clearly reflected the spiritual laws at work.

This chapter has been divided into three sections—Fall, Winter, and Spring—for the reader's convenience and because these three time periods did, in fact, represent developmentally distinct intervals in the group's life.

Fall

September classes began as this teacher had always begun—with establishment of class rules. She had traditionally prepared a lecture about the rules she felt were most important. Although pupil input was welcomed, it had served more as a supplement to the lecture than as its content. This year, the students' ideas were included to a greater extent.

The rules-discussion emphasis was set by the teacher; she asked for behaviors which the class had found most detrimental to learning. It had been the teacher's long-term observation that focusing only on positive behaviors and ignoring negative ones was counterproductive in a classroom of emotionally disturbed children. Deeply embedded in destructive behavior patterns which they are often unable to control, disturbed children are aided by an explicit identification of those behaviors which have, in effect, obscured their positive potentials. By clearly identifying the problem one externalizes it so that it can be handled. As long as the problem is unnamed, it remains an amorphous entity entertwined in the individual's notion of who he is. To destroy it, he may reason, he must destroy himself. It was this teacher's aim to show the pupils that their negative behaviors and attitudes were problems which they had embraced—and which they could—and should—release.

For these reasons problematic behaviors were identified, posted, and assigned points which would be deleted if the student engaged in them (see description of behavior-modification system, chapter 2). The behaviors were

1. Physical abuse
2. Verbal harassment
3. Willful destruction of property
4. Poor student behavior (such as speaking nastily, not attending to school assignments, not raising one's hand, talking and running in the hallways)
5. Failure to follow teacher direction (ignoring or refusing to comply with teacher requests)
6. Unnecessary little annoyances (such as tampering with the room speaker which connected to the principal's office, making distracting noises during quiet time)

September 18, Class Meeting

Issue. This first meeting, in which the classroom rules were established, is presented almost in its entirety to show the reader the process of rule installation.

Teacher: Rules in a society or rules in a classroom . . . What are we talking about? It seems that no matter what society you go into, whether it's in modern America or underdeveloped countries, wherever you go, even among animals, there's a set of rules. In every classroom you've been in, haven't you had rules? In our society we call rules "laws." Those of you I saw (for pretesting)—we talked about the laws of society, remember? Now—why do you think it's important to have rules?

Matthew: So things don't get carried away.

Teacher: So things don't get carried away.

Nicole: So people don't get hurt.

Teacher: So people don't get hurt.

Andrew: So there'll be no complaints.

Teacher: OK. Those are all very good reasons to have rules. What do you think a classroom would be like without any rules at all? Andrew?

Andrew: Impossible.

Teacher: Impossible. Nicole?

Nicole: Kids would be snotty.

Teacher: Kids would be snotty. Philip?

Philip: People would be screaming and fighting.

Teacher: People would be screaming and fighting. Would you learn very much?

Philip: No.

Teacher: No. So, that's why I always like, the very first thing, to talk about the rules. I'm glad that you agree with me that it's important that we have rules in a classroom, because it is. Otherwise, we can't learn anything and it it would be a waste of a year. I sat down last night and I thought of some things that were important in having a classroom run smoothly. I now want to know what kinds of things you don't like in a classroom. What kinds of things bother you? What kinds of things keep you from learning? And keep other people from learning? Would you raise your hand? John?

John: Screaming and fighting.

Teacher: Screaming and fighting. All right. I have something like that. I called fighting "physical abuse." When you abuse someone you treat him badly; and when you physically abuse someone, that means that you are physically hurting him. What are some other things that you can do besides hit someone to show him that you don't like what he's doing? Andrew?

Andrew: Profanity.

Teacher: Profanity. All right, you can cuss at him. What other things could you do besides cuss?

Nicole: Talk it out?

Teacher: Talk it out? All right. Is there anything else that you can do? Suppose someone does something to you and you are really angry and you don't want to cuss at him and you're too upset to really talk it out. What's something else you could do right at that moment? Keith?

Keith: Tell the teacher. Sometimes it's better that way.

Teacher: Tell the teacher. I agree. One thing I do want to make clear is that, if ever anything goes wrong, if you feel you've been wronged or something is not fair, would you please tell either the assistant or me? That's very important. I would rather you tell us than hit somebody or cuss at somebody. We will handle it, and if we can't handle it, we will get someone to help us handle it. But I would prefer that you tell us about it instead of just hauling off and hitting the person back, if that's the case. That will help to keep our classroom free from physical abuse. And, if you tell us, then we can deal with the person in another way. . . . Anything else that you've found makes a classroom a bad place to live in? Andrew?

Andrew: Back talking to the teacher.

Teacher: All right. I have a category for that too. Back talking to a teacher I called "failure to follow a teacher's direction." Boy, we're agreeing just beautifully so far about things that don't go well in a classroom. Why is it a problem when we fail to follow directions that the teacher gives us? Nicole?

Nicole: Because you're not following what the teacher says; like, if she tells you to sit down . . .

Teacher: And why is that a problem?

Nicole: Because, if everyone would do that, then the room would be just torn apart.

Teacher: Right. If everyone did that, then the room would be torn apart. The assistant and I will try to make reasonable demands upon you, like would you do your math, or would you be quiet, or would you line up at the door, or would you not cuss—things like that. Anything else that you find you just don't like in a room?

Students: (Silence)

Teacher: Well, I've got a few. Want me to tell you mine?

Student: OK.

Teacher: Harassment. Does anyone know what that word means? Harassment.

Carrie: Embarrass?

Teacher: Yes, harassment does embarrass people. Let me give you an example: Suppose someone in here does something that you don't like, and you know that you can't hit him in here.

Matthew: Harass him.

Teacher: Right. So, you say, "You just wait. When I get you outside, I'm going to do this, this, and this . . ." That definitely does not make for a very nice classroom, does it? Especially when you're sitting in your seat all day angry or worrying. You can't learn . . . This next one I put in because I've had problems with it two or three times the five years I've been teaching—not very often, but when there's a problem, there's a *real* problem. I'm calling it "willful destruction of property." What does that mean?

Matthew: Breaking something.

Teacher: Breaking something or stealing things.

Andrew: Destroying things.

Teacher: Destroying things. If you break something by accident, that's one thing, but actually walking over to something and breaking it . . .

Assistant: Writing on the desks.

Nicole: Writing on the walls.

Teacher: Yes.

Assistant: Chairs and things like that.

Teacher: Breaking things, stealing, writing on the desks and on the walls—just willful destruction of somebody's else's property. How would you feel if someone came into your house and started breaking things and writing on your walls and stealing your stuff? How do you feel when someone willfully destroys something that belongs to you?

Carrie: I'd feel bad. . . .

Keith: We're writing all these rules up; that doesn't mean that everybody's going to do that the whole year. That doesn't mean it's going to work the whole year. Problems are going to happen.

Teacher: Wouldn't it be marvelous if no problems did happen?

Keith: Yeah.

John: That would be a miracle.

Teacher: Do you think it is possible?

Keith: If everyone would mind their own business and did their own . . . maybe.

Teacher: Do you think we could try? I think we could try. I think we could possibly do it.

Assistant: If each one said to himself that he is going to do it, there's no problem.

Teacher: True. That's very true. If you would just control yourself there would be no problem.

Matthew: Um hum.

Teacher: If each person would control himself, we would have a beautiful classroom. I think we can . . . Now, are there any others?

Students: (Silence)

Teacher: I've got a couple little ones that I think we need to talk about. I call them "unnecessary little annoyances." For instance, you're sitting in class and everyone's supposed to be quiet and you're going (tapping pencil on the desk), and it drives everybody crazy.

Carrie: I know because I always do that. I got another one: fooling around with the speaker.

Teacher: That is an unnecessary little annoyance, yes. The speaker is connected to the main office and every time we lift it up it clicks up there . . . The last one I called "poor student behavior." What do you think will go under that category? Nicole?

Nicole: Cursing; not raising your hand.

Teacher: All right. Things like cursing; things like not raising your hand. Things like talking in the halls, because that disturbs other classes. Things like speaking to each other nastily.

Keith: These rules aren't going to work . . . like, if everybody else like mind their own business.

Teacher: Yes?

Keith: That's it—that everybody should mind their own business.

Analysis. The teacher had already formulated a list of rules gleaned from her previous five years of teaching emotionally disturbed children. It was interesting that these students identified the same problem behaviors (although not as many) as she had. Because the rules focused upon eliminating negative, disturbed behaviors, the discussion centered upon the consequences of engaging in them ("And why is that a problem?") and, in some instances, on alternative responses to situations which predictably elicited them ("What's something else you could do right at that moment?"). The teacher did not expand upon Nicole's suggestion to "talk it out" because experience had shown her that disturbed children, when upset, are ill inclined to rationalize. The teacher advocated the need for the rules in Stage–2 language when she asked the students to put themselves in the position of the person transgressed against ("How do you feel when someone willfully destroys something that belongs to you?"). It is to be noted that she was not happy to spend so much time discussing the "willful destruction of property" rule and was surprised at the extent of the conversation.

The students were worried about their collective ability to adhere to the classroom rules, and Keith proposed a norm of Mind Your Own Business as a way to reconcile the descrepancy between the "should" of compliance and the "would" of probable actual behaviors. The teachers offered a similar argument that each person should control himself.

Outcome. The formation of the rules alone was hardly sufficient to curb the students' highly disturbed behavior patterns. The rules had to be expanded and enforced again and again throughout the fall months.

Anecdotal Records

In September, as might be expected, highly disturbed behavior predominated. The students were unusually influenced by each other's behaviors and showed little ability to evaluate or to regulate trigger reactions to external stimuli. An event called forth a habitual behavioral response from each student, and because the class was composed exclusively of disturbed students, the response was reinforced by the problematic responses of others.

For example, on the second day of school, someone (Nicole) stole ten dollars from the teacher's purse. The teacher reported the theft to the class and announced that, to replace her loss, she would not finance their planned treat at the end of that week. Immediately, John (known the previous year as a compulsive thief) was suspected by several class members who had known him then. Although the teacher repeatedly asserted that no one could be accused without evidence, Philip, Keith, and Nicole initiated a sustained and intense attack on John which lasted for sixteen nightmarish days. Philip's habitual behavior pattern was one of physical violence; Nicole's was one of manipulation. Keith was known for his general delinquency.

Philip had decided upon John's guilt and was relentlessly abusing him physically; no amount of reasoning would make Philip stop. Keith teamed gleefully with Philip, more for the general enjoyment of the mischief than from any sense of righteousness. Nicole manipulated the aggressors and fanned the physical abuse by announcing that she had seen the ten dollars sticking out of John's back pocket on the bus. She was astute enough to know that Andrew, whose habitual behavior pattern was one of acquiescence to power and authority, would corroborate the lie—which he did. At the same time, John, whose habitual behavior pattern was to invite physical abuse, wouldn't stand up for his innocence quite convincingly enough.

Thus, the class reeled in violence and lies until the teacher one day struck Philip to stop his physical abuse. Although her job was threatened by Philip's parents, the abuse stopped and reason began to appear. Philip then noted that Nicole had been getting off the bus at an amusement park instead of at her customary bus stop every day for two weeks after the theft. The rest of the students then recalled that Nicole had bought extra desserts at lunch during that same period of time. In private, Nicole nodded ''yes'' to the teacher's expressed assumption of her guilt. The issue was resolved, but only after a severe struggle on the part of the teacher to break their destructively interwoven behavior patterns.

On October 5 during the scheduled dilemma discussion, the conversation was suddenly turned by Philip to the stealing incident:

Philip: All right, did John steal it? I'm not saying if he did . . .

Teacher: I said no.

Philip: He didn't?

Teacher: No.

Philip: I'm sorry John, for picking on you.

Student: Me too.

Student: I'm sorry.

Thomas: Man!

Philip: Who stole it?

Thomas: I don't care. I don't want . . . I ain't worrying about it. I don't care. Ten dollars doesn't mean nothing to me!

Teacher: The person who stole it . . . . I would appreciate them saying something about it one of these days.

Thomas: (disgustedly) Now everybody want to say ''sorry'' to John.

Although Philip already strongly suspected Nicole, it is hypothesized that he wanted a final confirmation from the teacher so that he could, in clear conscience, apologize to John. Several other students followed his lead.

From October until the middle of November the highly disturbed atmosphere of September was still in evidence. One antisocial act triggered like actions. Destruction of property, disturbing lunchroom behavior, violence, lack of group cohesion, bullying, and name calling were concerns. On October 6 someone knocked out an entire classroom window; the glass shattered on the macadam playground two stories below us, which mercifully had no children on it. (Matthew was sitting by the window at the time but denied the deed.) On that same day Philip unscrewed the spigot from the classroom sink, and someone unknown removed and hid the only knob to the art cabinet door. The teacher's reaction to this series of events was immediate and strong. That afternoon Thomas pointed out the doorknob which someone had mysteriously placed on her desk. Destructive acts stopped. It was during this period, too, that the extent and severity of Thomas's violent nature became apparent.

October 6, Class Meeting

Issue. During this meeting, two lunch-table policies which put an end to serious lunch-time problems originating solely within the group were firmly established. The first policy was made in reaction to Carrie's selfishly hoarding the class's lunch recess time. For days Carrie had taken so long to eat ice cream cones that the class (which was required to wait for her) was missing a significant part of its outside lunch recess. The assistant, who supervised the group during lunch time, raised the issue of Carrie's slow eating and suggested that she not be allowed to buy ice cream during lunch. Nicole alternately suggested that Carrie be allowed to buy ice cream but only on rainy days, when no one would be in a hurry to get outside. After much discussion the teacher and Keith proposed a policy which the class voted unanimously to accept:

Teacher: Well, we can't really say she can't have ice cream. We *can* say this: If you get ice cream, it must be finished by the time the rest of us go out or we . . .

Assistant: Throw it away.

Teacher: Or we throw it away.

Keith: You're right, Teacher. Throw it away. Like, when everybody else is done, or we all should have to be done at a certain time. It doesn't even take ten minutes to eat. So, we all should have eight minutes to eat or something like that.

Teacher: Can we set a time when everyone has to go outside?

Thomas: Yeah! Yeah! I was just thinking of that!

Teacher: Can we set a time? Can we say by 11:15, anyone . . .

Students: Yep. Yep.

Teacher: . . . anyone who's not finished will have to forfeit what he's eating?

Issue. The second policy was made in reaction to Matthew's ill-mannered lunch-table eating habits. Matthew recently had rubbed two cupcakes together and spat out some food he didn't like. In this meeting the students expressed a deep dissatisfaction with his behavior:

Student: You're a pig eater!

Carrie: It's sick!

Philip: I feel like just punching him in his face.

Keith: Yeah, he's weird.

Peter: Like, it's embarrassing to the class. He's sitting there with his cupcakes, rubbing them together.

John: I feel embarrassed because when other kids look and see how he eats . . .

Nicole: And people are looking at him and I feel embarrassed. Our principal is looking at him and the principal of the other school is looking at him, too.

Matthew reacted to the students' displeasure first by denying his actions, threatening his accusers, and becoming defensive; then by announcing his intention and right to do whatever he wanted with his food. The following is a sequential list of his statements:

Matthew: I don't spit out my food. I'll beat your head in . . . If you don't shut up I'm going to go over there and make you shut up . . . No I don't . . . You'd better shut up, girl! . . . Why is everybody always jumping on my back? . . . If I want to I will . . . Well, so what, it's my cake and I . . . They can't choose what I have for lunch.

Matthew's responses elicited a norm which had been applied, on occasion, to intractable students in the classroom before—that is, Separate the Deviant Member(s) from the Group:

Teacher: All right, we've already established the fact that people are embarrassed, it makes them sick, and they don't like the way Matthew is eating. Now, the next thing we have to discuss is, what does Matthew intend to do about it? Matthew?

Matthew: Nothing.

Teacher: What are we going to do about it now that Matthew says he refuses to change his eating habits?

Philip: Make him eat alone.

Teacher: How many people think that's a good suggestion? One, two, three, four, five, six. How many people think that it's not a good suggestion? One. All right, the person who disagrees may speak.

Only Keith opposed taking this action; he reproposed an alternative norm of Mind Your Own Business (the same norm he had proposed during the rules discussion in September):

Keith: I don't know why he's embarrassing us guys. He's making a fool of himself. Let him make a fool of himself. That don't mean that we should make him sit at another table or something.

The norm remained in the proposal phase, however, because the class's vote to separate Matthew from them at the lunch table held.

Matthew was incensed at this vote. In explaining to Matthew the necessity of the voted-upon action, the teacher asked him to act like a good member of the group by altering his eating habits. Matthew had no intention of modifying his behavior to meet group standards, however; and he continued to deliver threats to the class members who had voted "against" him:

Teacher: Well, Matthew, the situation is that you really annoy the other people sitting at the table. People are asking you if you are willing to give a little bit of yourself—to act like a member of the group, and eat correctly when you eat at the table. You point-blank said "No," so what else are we supposed to do? You have left us no other choice. We either have to sit there and look at you being a poor member of the group or we have to ask you to eat someplace else. Now, what else can we do? If you have another option, Matthew, tell us. People do not want to ignore you because they say it's too hard to ignore. Whatever it is you do, it's very annoying . . .

Matthew: . . . flattened out. Your face is going to look like . . . I'll kill you.

Analysis. To summarize the meeting in developmental terms, the class had clearly become a group with minimal collective normative expectations: (1) class members should cooperate by ending their lunch in time to have a full lunch recess, and (2) class members should eat with manners at the lunch table (Norm: Eat with Manners).

The first normative expectation indicated that the class shared a Stage–2, Phase–2 sense of community. All members were to be guaranteed equal eating and play time; no one person had the right to take more than his fair share of either. The class members accepted the institution of this policy through vote.

The norm Eat with Manners was evidently well established by this meeting, for it was here being presented at Phase 5 and 6b. The community expressed its deep displeasure with Matthew's eating habits and reported his violation of the norm publicly. It is probable that this norm had already been a part of most of the students' behavioral repertoires prior to their entry into this classroom.

The norm Separate the Deviant Member(s) from the Group was upheld by all members but Keith through a vote. Such strong support for the norm places it solidly at Phase 2, acceptance. Because no student reasoning for its acceptance was probed by the teacher, it is not possible to assign the norm a stage.

Peter, John, and Nicole offered Stage–3 reasons in support of the norm. They were sensitive to how the class looked to other people: "It's embarrassing to the class."

Keith reintroduced the alternative Stage–2 norm Mind Your Own Business which, as previously noted, remained at proposal Phase 1.

Outcome. The discussion of Matthew's eating habits had a positive effect. Matthew sufficiently modified his behavior and never did have to be separated from the group.

October 13, Class Meeting

Issues. This class meeting focused upon two major issues: the misbehavior of a subgroup during music class and the nasty way in which Philip had been talking to the teacher.

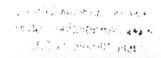

Some of the students had been acting so poorly during music that the music teacher had threatened to split the class and to teach half the students at a time. The teacher strongly opposed this move because she wanted the group to learn to work together.

Teacher: You put me in a really bad situation in music. The music teacher was going to split our class up—like kindergarten kids; like we are really crazy. He was going to take only four kids at a time, which I think is ridiculous, because at our age we need to learn how to sit through music as a group all at once.

Andrew: Yes.

Teacher: The point is, we're here and we're all supposed to be getting ready to go back to a regular classroom. And one of the things about going back to a regular classroom is, whether you like the subject or not, if it's scheduled, that's what you have to go and do. You have no right to act up and interrupt and spoil everyone else's time. There are some things that each of us doesn't like about the school day. Some people don't like the math part; some people don't especially like gym; some people don't like the music part; and yet, is it right for a person, just because he doesn't happen to like a particular subject, to disrupt so no one else can enjoy it either?. . . . Life isn't perfect and neither is school. There are certain times you have to sit through things that you don't particularly like. I think it's babyish not to be able to sit through forty-five minutes a week of something that you don't especially like. I'm not asking you to like it and neither is anyone else. We're just asking you to consider other people in this classroom that exist besides just you, and behave yourself in music. Grow up a little. All right? You're calling yourselves older, and yet your behavior was like that of very young children. All I'm asking you to do, and other people in here are asking you to do, is to act your age. If you don't like it, participate anyway. It's forty-five minutes; it's once a week. And if you can't take that much aggravation, then you haven't grown up.

Two students supported the teacher's arguments—Andrew, in his supportive "Yes" in the entry above, and Nicole:

Nicole: The way we acted *was* terrible. If they don't like music, they don't have to mess it up for everybody. 'Cause, maybe someone would like to have his own career in music, and he wants to learn.

John, Peter, and Thomas, however, did not accept the teacher's argument that the class should remain as a group during music. They reiterated the norm Separate the Deviant Member(s) from the Group:

Peter: You know, they should stay out.

John: They should stay out and walk upstairs and do their work—their morning folder work, and do math . . .

Thomas: Whatever. As long as they're out, man.

The teacher refused to agree to this and, insisted that the group remain intact during music class and act its age while there. No vote was taken.

Analysis. Two norms were proposed by the teacher during the discussion of this issue: Act Your Age and Take Other Class Members into Account. Only one student supported each norm. Andrew agreed with the first; Nicole offered an argument for the second. For this reason, the norms remained in the proposal phase.

Both norms were supported by Stage–3 arguments. The teacher held up a prosocial, normative model of early-adolescent behavior—the ability to participate in any standard school activity without incident. She then proceeded to explain what it was that allowed the normal junior-high-aged student to do this: the ability to take other people's feelings or positions into account in any given situation and to accommodate the self's behavior accordingly. This ability was critical to a successful experience in a regular classroom.

Outcome. The class was not split up for music class.

Issue. The second issue was also introduced by the teacher. Philip had been asking her for help with his workbooks during the morning work hours. As soon as the teacher would begin to help him, however, he would storm away and speak to her nastily. The teacher was distraught and asked the students for their help in dealing with Philip:

Teacher: I think this is something we need to talk about. I can't run a class like this. I cannot tolerate it, and I want to know what you think ought to be done. I feel that I have been wrongly treated because he yelled and talked to me nastily yesterday and today when I was trying to help him with work. He came over to me to ask me to help him, and when I went to help him he started speaking to me nastily. I don't like it. It really makes me angry because I haven't even done anything to him to set him off. He can't go back to a regular classroom like that. A regular classroom teacher won't tolerate it. So, it's not good for him and it's not good for me, and I want to know what it is that I can do, or you can do . . .

John: He doesn't bully me.

Peter: *You* should just settle it. It's not our problem.

John: I know, man.

Nicole: It isn't our problem.

Teacher: You don't think it's your problem?

Peter: No, he's the one who's hurting you.

Andrew: He behaves the way he always has.

Teacher: You think I should handle it.

Nicole: It isn't our problem.

John: It's not our problem.

Peter: It's not our problem.

Teacher: Does anyone have any reasonable suggestions?

John: No. It's not our problem, so why should we get into it?

Peter: He's not the one who's calling us the names.

Andrew: He's hurting you more than he's hurting us.

The teacher countered these answers by appealing to the students' stake in supporting the well-being of all members in the class by virtue of their own classroom membership:

Teacher: But it's your classroom. You're in the classroom.

This made no impression:

Peter: It's not our classroom.

At this, the teacher appealed to their Stage–2 concrete-exchange sense of justice. The students then responded, but with Stage–2 authoritarian and physicalistic (Matthew and Carrie) solutions:

Teacher: Shoot. I'm the one who stands up and helps you when someone bothers you. When Matthew was eating in the lunchroom, he
wasn't bothering me, but I sat here and I gave suggestions, and so,
now when I'm asking for . . .

Nicole: OK, I have a suggestion . . .

Andrew: All right. Take him down to the principal's office for the rest
of the day.

Peter: Call his parents.

Thomas: Well, *that's* going to stop it.

Student: Suspend him. . . .

Matthew: Send him to the Germans . . .

Carrie: Smack him across his face.

Matthew: Yeah, put a star on him and send him to the Germans.

Analysis. Clearly, the students did not care about the teacher's problem.
They spoke in terms of "we" and "you" ("It isn't *our* problem." "He's
hurting *you* more than he's hurting *us.*") indicating that they shared a
sense of student unity and that they viewed the teacher as an authority
separate from them who should do her job ("You should just settle it")
but for whom they had no personal responsibility.

This was probably a Stage–2 interchange because of the emphasis
on each "part" being responsible for itself. No value of community was
apparent ("It's not our classroom.")

Of particular interest during this meeting was the interaction between
this teacher and Philip:

Teacher: He can have his free time here, not with me, because he can't
ask me to like him when he acts that way, and I've . . .

Philip: I ain't asking you to like me.

Teacher: . . . and I've watched you with other kids, on the bus and on the playground—and you treat everybody nastily.

Philip: I guess I do.

Teacher: Yes, you do. I want to ask Philip . . .

Philip: Well, I ain't saying nothing.

Teacher: I want to discuss it anyway. I want to ask Philip why it is, yesterday and today, when he came over to me to give me work to help him with, that when I went to help him with it, he got so nasty?

Philip: (Silence)

Teacher: Is it because you don't know why you do that?

Philip: (Silence)

Teacher: Is it because you have no control over your own temper? Do you just blow up for no reason, usually?

Philip: (Silence)

Teacher: What are you thinking about when you come over and ask me to help you with your work and then start screaming at me?

Philip: (Silence)

Teacher: If you don't want help, then why do you walk over and ask me to help you?

Philip: (Silence)

Teacher: It doesn't make any sense to me, and it's not at all reasonable behavior. Why don't you tell me what you want to be done here, Philip?

Philip: (Silence)

Teacher: We don't have to talk. I'll collect your work and correct it after school and give it to you to correct, and you can pick it up any way you want to. We can do it that way. I won't teach you one-on-one. I'll write you notes, if that's the way it's got to be. We won't talk. I'd prefer not to talk to you at all than to have you speak like that. Now what is it that you want to do about it?

Philip: (Silence)

Andrew: She's asking you, Philip.

Philip: (Silence)

Teacher: I'm asking you a reasonable question.

Philip: (Silence)

Teacher: I'm asking you a reasonable question and you're giving me no answer, which means that you must not have anything to say about your behavior.

Philip: (Silence)

Teacher: You must not have any justification.

Outcome. For the time being, Philip quit interacting with the teacher in a confrontative manner. Both the teacher and the assistant praised him at the end of the week for having been a "model" student.

Anecdotal Records

Ascending during this period were Stage–2 subgroups which functioned to a great extent as protection from aggressors, both from within and outside of the classroom. John, Peter, and Matthew were the first students to form such a group during outside lunch recess. The assistant had brought in a frisbee, which they had adopted as their recess activity. Both the teacher and the assistant were pleased with the trio; however rudimentary and pragmatic the reasons for its formation may have been, it was the first group to form around a socially appropriate activity. The harmonious trio was soon assailed, however, by Thomas, who wanted to join their game. The subgroup promptly spurned his advances. This fanned Thomas's anger, and predictably, he turned on John (the perpetual victim) who ran around the school building to escape Thomas and refused to come inside.

The extreme difficulty in handling Thomas arose, in part, from the impacted intensity and the duration of his smoldering anger and violence. By the time everyone but John had come inside, Thomas's anger was in full force and was not to be stemmed. In the classroom he refused to sit down or to go downstairs to the crisis-classroom teacher. He assumed his now-familiar angry prowling around the classroom, awaiting his prey— John. When Thomas was in such a temper, no one in the building could or would try to restrain him physically. (The two men teachers had informed the principal in September that they would not be available for this.)

John came into the building with another class and entered the room; as soon as Thomas saw him, he leaped to the attack. John, quick on his feet, flew back out of the room and down the hall. This teacher grabbed Thomas by the shirt, which tore as he strained to break away. They tussled briefly and when it came clear that he would have to strike her to get away, Thomas held back from this final defiance and agreed to go to the crisis classroom (where he would be pampered and given candy). John returned to the room.

Half an hour later, supposedly having been calmed down, Thomas was sent to the classroom to gather his things in preparation for being sent home. He burst through the door, threw his desk and his chair across the room, crossed the room himself, and swept everything off the assistant's desk onto the floor. At that, he turned on his heels, grabbed his bookbag and stomped out of the room. The class sat stunned, heads turning in unison as all eyes followed Thomas's rampage. As soon as he was gone, Nicole and Matthew jumped up and restored everything to its proper place. Thomas returned to the class the next school day, acting quite pleasantly.

The issue of subgrouping and violence continued. Thomas, always the major aggressor, repeatedly tried to force his way into a group and ignored agreed-upon classroom rules in his foiled attempts to do so. By the beginning of November, for instance, dyads were well established in the playing of ''Battleship,'' an inside strategy game. The class had passed a rule that there were to be no bystanders while two people were playing, because a bystander would often reveal one person's ship locations and ruin the game. Everyone had understood the need for such a rule and had unanimously voted to instate it; people had been playing for several days without incident.

One morning Thomas walked over to watch a game in progress. The teacher reminded him of the rule and asked him to move; he stood immobile and silent. She asked again, reminding him of the agreed-upon rule; again, he neither answered her nor budged from his spot. An argument ensued which escalated—Thomas once again reverting to an animalistic anger. The teacher managed to persuade Thomas to leave the classroom with her for the crisis room downstairs. All the way down the stairs he tried to taunt her into a physical confrontation. When that failed, he began to slow suddenly in his movements as if hoping to catch the teacher offguard and have her bump into him. By this date, however, the teacher was well aware of the need for hawk—like vigilance when interacting with this student and paced herself carefully, avoiding the violence that was waiting.

She was unable to avert the violence entirely, however. The crisis teacher, afraid of what she saw in Thomas, left the teacher with him in the crisis classroom and went to get the principal. The crisis teacher and principal remained outside of the room for some time as Thomas and the teacher argued about his right to act the way that he had, entering only when he forcefully threw two solid metal trucks at this teacher's head— barely missing it.

Needless to say, this teacher was furious at the interchange. She announced to the principal her heart-felt disinclination to attend that evening a previously scheduled dinner at the group home where Thomas was housed. She felt strongly that Thomas should feel the consequences of his behavior; when a person treats someone with contempt and violence, he shouldn't be rewarded. How was Thomas to learn to change if he was denied the natural consequences of his actions? (The teacher was repelled by the prospect of having to go against a universal law— the law of cause and effect. By denying Thomas the opportunity to experience that truth, he was being denied the chance to modify his behavior and therefore, to function in human society.)

The principal did not agree. She argued that Thomas was behaving as he was because he felt a close personal relationship with the teacher— who was black, as was Thomas—and needed her love and understanding. She then all but ordered the teacher to appear at the dinner that evening as planned. This teacher complied and attended the dinner (where Thomas displayed his loveliest side), but the basic wrongness of her act rankled within her. To reward an evil is not love.

Meanwhile, the rest of the class was moving sporadically toward cohesiveness, although not enough trust had been formed between them to support mutual sharing of their most serious personal concerns. Trust in the teacher did exist, however; and private conferences were scheduled with her. Peter initiated this trend on October 30, and it was immediately adopted by the other class members. Several hours of several consecutive days were spent in private conferences. In one such conference Peter expressed concern about the class's negative reaction to his effeminate behavior and asked for help. He and the teacher agreed upon a signaling system in which the teacher would pull her ear lobe whenever she noticed his acting overtly effeminate. This system was instituted; Peter modified his more blatant actions; his group standing improved.

Perhaps the strongest indicator of the class's move toward cohesiveness was a discussion about grouping for games on the playground. Also, the disturbing behavior of Philip, which resurfaced and affected everyone by this time, brought the class together in protest. Both concerns were issues in the November 3 class meeting.

November 3, Class Meeting

Issue. Andrew had been claiming the class ball for solitary basketball practice every day at lunch recess. No one else had expressed an interest in using the ball or in joining Andrew until the beginning of November. At that time, the teacher spoke to him about the need to share the ball. Andrew resisted this for reasons which are quoted in the next exchange:

Teacher: Let me give you some background on this. It first came to my attention about three days ago when someone said he wanted to play with the class ball—that Andrew wasn't letting anyone else play with it. I told Andrew that the ball belonged to the class and that he couldn't keep it to himself the whole time. He told me that he didn't want to share it with the class because the class didn't know how to play with it correctly. Since you didn't know how to play with it correctly, you shouldn't really use it; and since he was the one who knew how to play with it, he should. We got into a long conversation in which I said that whether or not the class knew how to play with it correctly according to Andrew's standards didn't make any difference, because the ball still belonged to the class as a whole; he had no right to take the ball for himself only. I was hoping that the class would follow that up and say, well, they *did* want to play, and we would figure out some schedule. But then, when I brought it to your attention a couple of days ago everyone said, "Well, just let him play with it."

Peter, John, and Thomas proposed that individuals take turns using the class ball during lunch recess:

Peter: Well, everybody gets a day for the ball. All right, it's Monday— Andrew gets it. Then he gets to give it to the next person Tuesday.

Thomas: Yeah! Then, if they don't want it, you can let someone else use it.

John: The line leader [which changes daily] uses it.

The assistant then presented an alternative solution in which the group (with the exception of Andrew) would play together and, as a group, alternate days with Andrew:

Assistant: It doesn't make sense for each of you to be a loner with the ball. The class should play kickball some days and Andrew can play basketball alone on others.

This was the first time anyone had suggested that the entire class (except Andrew, who was single-mindedly pursuing a career as a professional basketball player) play together during free recess time. The suggestion remained a proposal, however. No one was ready to do this.

Peter then proposed a solution which did appeal and which the class voted unanimously to accept: Divide the class into interest groups— kickball and basketball. Each day a vote would be taken to determine how many people wanted to play either one. The activity with the most people would win the class ball.

Analysis. In the discussion of this issue, the assistant and the teacher argued, but probably at different stages, that the class should operate as a unit (The Group is One). The assistant proposed that individuals should not function independently of each other but should play as a group on the playing field; the teacher argued that the class ball be shared fairly by all class members.

These arguments are difficult to stage. It could be said that the teacher was advocating the institution of a Stage–2 system of concrete, instrumental exchange: ''and we would figure out some schedule.'' Peter reflected this in his first proposal to have the ball rotate among individual students: ''Well, everybody gets a day for the ball.'' The assistant then criticized the individual system of instrumental exchange—''It doesn't make sense for each of you to be a loner with the ball''—and proposed that the class play together. It could be argued that the assistant's proposal more closely approximated Stage 3. It was not fully Stage 3, however, because no mention was made of creating a caring, friendly interactive unit on the playing field—only that the students should take the first step of getting together there.

In response to this, Peter proposed that the class should split into subgroups that shared the same interest. While this proposal was a move away from Stage–2 individualism, it was hardly an advocation of a Stage–3 caring, familial unit. It may well be that Peter's proposal remained at Stage 2 and that his reason for suggesting (and the class's reason for accepting) it was based on the Stage–2 understanding of one's instrumental need for the other: to play ball on the playing field.

Outcome. The class did not share the class ball. Andrew kept it, and the rest played games that did not require its use. Nicole, John, and Peter, in particular, had formed a playing subground and played tag every day.

Issue. Philip's violent behavior had become a concern of every class member by November; he was no longer confining his belligerence to his dealings with adults or to isolated students but was directing it toward everyone. In this meeting the class tried to discuss the problem with Philip.

Teacher: Well, I've been having a lot of trouble with you this week— this whole week.

Nicole: Philip, everybody's been having problems with you. Even everybody said it.

Students: (Silence)

Nicole: Everybody's just ascared to say because you . . .

Philip: Why don't you just drop dead.

Teacher: No, all right, I'll start. What's been bothering me this week is that you don't do any of your work . . .

Philip: I do my work! Don't tell me I don't!

Teacher: You fool around a lot. You have separated yourself basically from the class, and from a kid that used to be well controlled and used to hate behavior that was . . .

Matthew: (under his breath) mentally retarded . . .

Philip responded to Matthew's comment by forcefully knocking Matthew and his chair backwards. Philip was sent to the crisis classroom, and the class members were most solicitous of the howling Matthew. In the discussion that followed, the students criticized Philip's Stage–1 inability to take what he gave out and Nicole described his Stage–1 terrorism on the bus:

Teacher: I want to know what's going on with Philip because I've noticed this week he has changed into another person.

Andrew: Every time Philip calls somebody a name, the guy answers him—calls him a jerk off—*after* Philip has called him a name—Philip just beats him up.

Teacher: Philip can call other people names. He does it all the time.

Peter: But nobody else can call him a name.

Nicole: And Philip's always coming over and hitting me, and I hit him back and then he gets real mad. There's one thing I don't like. He comes on the bus, you know . . .

John: Man, you can't even say *nothing* on the bus. He'll tell you to be quiet.

Nicole: We were talking—having our voice up—and Philip said, "Shut up! Shut up!" I said, "Philip, they're allowed to talk if they want." And he goes, "Shut up, you bitch!" I said, "Your mother." Then he kept on calling my mom all kinds of names. One day, when we were driving him home, when he gets off, this kid was sitting right up here. Philip just went right after him and started punching him in the face.

Suggested solutions were predictable: remove Philip from the class altogether, separate him from the others within the classroom, tell his parents.

Analysis. The class was criticizing Philip's lack of Stage–2 ability (1) to stand outside of himself and take a second-person perspective and (2) to see that how he treated others determined to a great extent how others treated him. Philip's actions reflected the Stage–1 belief that "might makes right," that the strong control the weak, and that the weak should be obedient. In its criticism, the class demonstrated its Stage–2 sense of community valuing.

Outcome. Three days after this meeting, Philip witnessed two children being hit and killed by an oncoming train. Philip reported the incident during Sharing Time (another child corroborated its occurrence) and said that it had upset him deeply. Over the next two days it gradually occurred to this teacher that Philip had attracted that violent event. The violent energy he had been spewing into his environment all week had contacted like energy. For every effect there is a cause; like attracts like. She shared her thoughts with Philip. She told him that if he wished to attract pleasantness to himself, he would have to send out corresponding vibrations. Philip exhibited visible relief at this advice—he let out a sigh and his whole body relaxed.

Anecdotal Records

A major, vocalized concern of the teacher's had been the nasty way in which class members talked to each other. The students would fill any time not programmed by the adults with insulting comments. The teacher would always identify the negative nature of the conversation and exhort the students to be pleasant to each other, but it wasn't until the end of October that her efforts had any visible effect. Then, the students began to make obvious effort to be more pleasant to each other. On October 25, while the class was working on Halloween masks, for the first time since the beginning of the year the room was not filled with disgusting, insulting conversation. The teacher praised the class. On October 26 Matthew proudly announced that he and two other children had had a decent conversation at lunch recess.

Pupils also began to support the prosocial actions of class members and to value the class. On November 9 they congratulated Matthew for earning 200 perfect behavior-modification points for the first time all year. Unfortunately, he could not maintain this standard. On November 11, Peter, Andrew, and John welcomed a very-disturbed Matthew back into their music group and helped him to regain his mental stability by caringly and painstakingly teaching him what he had missed during the time he had had to be removed from music class. On November 15 Nicole came to school physically ill after her mother had left for work, having instructed her to stay home. Evidently the classroom had assumed major importance in her life. Also on November 15 during the class meeting, the issue of name calling was raised.

November 15, Class Meeting

Issue. The class accused Andrew of name calling and expressed its disapproval. After a heated discussion in which Andrew tried to deny his guilt, Peter admitted to engaging in the same offensive activity. Soon most of the class confessed that they, too, had been engaging in tit-for-tat name calling and that they didn't like it.

Until this time the class had had an unwritten policy to ignore name calling; now that policy had become no longer serviceable. The students didn't know what new to do about the transgressors, however, so they turned to the teacher for help. She suggested the following system:

Teacher: If three people hear the name being called, then I would like to take points off. What do you think about that? I say three people, because, if three people say something is happening, there's less likelihood of someone's lying about it.

This suggestion was not adopted by the class at this meeting, possibly because Philip expressed the concern that people might "gang up" and falsely accuse someone. This fear had been reinforced by four of the class members' (Philip's, John's, Andrew's, Nicole's) bus experience. Jude, their bus driver, had been exhorting Philip, John, and Andrew to hold Nicole in line:

John: Our bus driver, Jude, doesn't even like Nicole. Because, know what? If he did like Nicole, would he say, "Why don't you stick together, you guys, when she does something wrong; you tell me, right? If she does something wrong." Why would he say that if he liked Nicole? Jude's asking us boys to keep together.

Andrew: And even some people on the bus hate Nicole for what she's done.

The teacher responded to these remarks by asking the entire class to come together in care:

Teacher: Well, I would like to ask if you think it's possible for you to act as a cohesive group that cares about each other and will quit calling names. I'm asking the whole class, including Nicole, to stick together.

Vote. The class reluctantly voted to uphold the poorly functioning Ignore-Name-Calling norm because no other solution was acceptable to them at this time.

Analysis. The students expressed a dissatisfaction with the Stage–2 divisive atmosphere caused by name calling and began to explore ways to eliminate it. They did not trust each other enough, however, to accept the teacher's proposal of taking points from a name caller if three people reported him; to work successfully, this system depended upon the goodwill of class members toward each other (Stage–3 community valuing). Thus, they were thrown back on the Ignore-Name-Calling norm which had failed them (Phase 4).

Outcome. The agreed-upon policy to ignore name calling was not strong enough to eliminate it. The issue was raised again at the December 1 Class Meeting, and the teacher's original suggestion to delete points from the name caller if three people heard him call a name was spontaneously accepted and enforced by the class.

Anecdotal Records

Gym was the single activity in which negativity, factionalism, and divisiveness were rarely in evidence. From the beginning, the class played together beautifully in gym. Here they were able to set aside their personal animosities and disturbances, to compromise and coordinate and to unite in the attainment of a single end—to win. And win they did. From September to June, through serious, defeating problems in many areas of the class's life, it remained undefeated on the playing field. No group could beat it—no matter what combination of players from various classes the gym teacher put together or what handicap was imposed upon it, the class won every time.

Into the middle of November crept an evil, divisive influence which temporarily destroyed the positive cohesion that had been building among the class members and which seriously challenged the power of the teacher. In addition, it threatened the future of at least one class member. As previously mentioned, four of the seven children (Philip, Nicole, Andrew, and John) rode on the same school bus under the aegis of a bus driver named Jude. Unknown to this teacher, Jude had played the major role in the partial destruction of a classroom the previous year. He had "adopted" a child from one of the most disturbed classes; had filled him with a deep dissatisfaction with the school, his teacher, and his classwork; and had fueled the mounting rebellion of this child against them. As a result, the student left the school before the year was over, leaving a disrupted class which, reportedly, never fully recovered. (Details were not given to this author.)

This year Jude had "adopted" Philip. From the beginning of the year Philip had engaged in violent, angry, surly behaviors and had resisted being taught. After strong countering from the teacher, however, his negative behaviors would subside and he would go through days of showing positive effort. Now, in the middle of November, he settled into an entrenched anger and resentment about the "low" level of his schoolwork. He insisted on having higher level academic materials and steadfastly refused to acknowledge the empirical evidence that he could not function there.

His first complaint was about math. Andrew was in a higher math book than he. Despite the fact that he had not mastered the material in the book he was in, Philip refused to continue in it and demanded to be placed in the same book as Andrew. When the teacher pointed out the mistakes Philip had made in his own math book, problem for problem, he stated that the work was easy and that he knew how to do it. The teacher answered, "Then do it correctly and you can move on." To this Philip replied, "Andrew's father must be paying you to give him eighth-grade work!" Further discussion proved fruitless.

As a last resort, the teacher decided to appeal to the principal, sure of the principal's support of her position. Right before leaving for the principal's office, Philip gathered his hat, coat, and lunch in a clear statement of his determination to leave the class if his request was not granted. The principal's verdict came as a surprise to this teacher. She instructed the teacher to give Philip any material he wanted. Later she told this teacher that Jude had "adopted" Philip, that it was useless to try to resist Jude's influence, that the teacher should let Philip do whatever he could and simply forget about the rest.

The immediate results of the acquiescence on the part of the teacher were destructive. Philip gloated, paired with Thomas in sleeping through the afternoon class activity, and started verbally deriding Andrew as being "perfect." Peter and John, on the other hand, teamed up in a very positive way and worked together for most of the day. Within five days, however, Peter began to complain that *his* math was "too easy" and had to be shown otherwise.

Although Philip had good days, overall his behavior deteriorated. The work he had insisted on having was entirely too difficult for him. He worked alone, asking no one for help. Indeed, no one could help him without reintroducing the academic groundwork he had refused to do. Philip did not bear his predicament stoically. On the contrary, he became more violent and difficult than ever.

Jude had assigned to Philip the position of law enforcement officer on the bus, a position he had been fulfilling more or less since the end of October. His reign of power had become terrorism by the end of November. Philip's abuse of power on the bus was creating a serious problem between Nicole and him. Nicole, who was quite powerful in her own right, bitterly resented Philip's assigned lordship over her on the bus (see November 3 Class Meeting). At one point, tensions were so high between them that Nicole, whom this teacher had never known to back down from any challenge, gratefully accepted the suggestion that she stay inside with the teacher during lunch recess to avoid further confrontation with Philip.

Academically, Philip instituted an intense competitive battle between Andrew and himself. Both would race through the pages in their math books, seeing which one would get the farthest. Mistakes were no hindrance. By the afternoon the intensity would have built to such a pitch that Philip would degenerate into a negative, attacking attitude and draw in one or two other students with him.

By the end of November the competitive attitude had spread to several other class members. Nicole attacked John on the bus one day because he had used the time she had engaged in a tantrum to surpass her in his math book (they were in the same math group). The next morning on the bus Andrew had teamed with her, and upon leaving the bus they chased John through the neighborhood.

As can be seen, the surrender to the evil influence of Jude had spread throughout the classroom the disease he carried. The teacher could not fight effectively enough because her administration had refused to back her and because the seed of the difficulty (Jude) was out of her reach.

Clear progress was being made in one area. A subgroup of Nicole, Peter, Matthew and John had formed. They played ball together daily during lunch recess, and all but Matthew closely identified with each other in the classroom. Headed and molded by the strong-minded Nicole on the playing field, and softened and humanized by the sensitive Peter and John in the classroom, this group was the first to come close to interacting in a Stage–3 manner. It is suspected by this author that this group was a reaction, in part, to the relentless aggression of Philip and Thomas.

Although the subgroup of Nicole, Peter, and John was a real advance in classroom interactions, they experienced problems learning to work together in harmony. An example of their difficulties is presented in the December 1 Class Meeting.

December 1, Class Meeting

Issue. Nicole, Peter, Matthew, and John had been playing kickball daily during lunch recess. Nicole was the far-superior athlete and the most-forceful personality. When it was Peter's, John's, or Matthew's turn to kick, he would kick the ball from Nicole's area on the field. Although the boys never did admit the reason for their behavior, anyone who saw the group at play would understand: Nicole was so fast that if she had a running chance at the ball, no one would be able to make a base.

John: I got something to say about this. Outside playing kickball, Nicole starts to get real mad and all and starts . . . When it was her turn to be up and she came over to kick, she came and almost pushed me in the mud.

Peter: True.

John: And I don't think that's fair; and she called Peter and Matthew a "fairy."

Student: I'm a witness. I witnessed this.

Peter: Yeah. Respect! From Nicole. . . .

John: She got so mad, nobody was kicking it over to her. That's why we weren't . . .

Nicole: No, you knew you could kick it over to Matthew and Peter because they can't catch that good!

Student: Well, that's taking advantage.

Nicole: Yeah, I know. . . .

Peter: We'll be nice to her if she'll be nice to us.

John: Let's vote on it. If we be nice to . . .

Nicole: I ain't *never* going to be nice to you anymore, you . .

Analysis. This interchange evidenced a mixture of Stage–2 and Stage–3 reasoning. Peter and John, exhorting Nicole to treat them with respect and to be nice to them by not physically abusing them and calling them names, used Stage–3 reasoning to support their unfair treatment of her. Nicole countered the boys by exhorting them to recognize her concrete individual right (Stage 2) to have an opportunity to interact with the ball on the playing field.

Outcome. The subgroup continued to meet daily on the playing field and to struggle to establish a Stage–3 family unit.

Issue. The No-Name-Calling policy suggested by the teacher at the November 15 Class Meeting was spontaneously accepted at this meeting and put into practice:

Peter: Teacher. You said that when a person calls you a name and three people hear it that you'll take points away from him?

Teacher: Yes.

Peter: And John . . . Well, there's more than three of us that heard what Nicole called him.

Matthew: Yep!

Teacher: That is true. I got reports from three people, and points shall be taken for it.

Andrew: There were more than three people.

Teacher: (taking points) That's fifteen points.

Students: (clapping)

Analysis. The No-Name-Calling norm was operating at Phase 3. The students' decision to accept and immediately to enforce the teacher's more stringent deterrent was an indication that they expected the norm to be upheld.

Outcome. Name calling was not again an issue until March 4, when the students approved an even stronger policy of deterrence.

Issue. December added a fresh problem to the already overburdened classroom. A new student—Wayne—entered. Wayne had been on homebound instruction since September because he had physically attacked a teacher the previous year. The principal of Valley Brook felt he should be institutionalized, but state law required that he be placed first in this interim situation. As preparation for his entry, the teacher announced in this class meeting that a new student was soon to arrive, and she asked how he should be treated.

Nicole: Like, give him the milky treatment.

Peter: Like, show him around.

(Matthew is giggling and making incoherent comments.)

Andrew: Courteous.

Teacher: Courteous.

Andrew: Show him what to do at the lunch table.

(Matthew still giggling and commenting.)

Teacher: What about when we go outside to play games?

John: He's not going to like it.

Nicole: Let him join.

Teacher: Let him join.

John: He's not going to like it very much if somebody starts . . . We don't know how he's going to feel if somebody just stops in the middle of the game. We don't know how he's going to feel.

Philip: Man, we don't know how he's going to feel when Nicole's hollering and hollering and hollering.

John: Yeah, we don't know how he feels. We don't know what he likes to do.

Peter: Yeah, we don't know how he's going to feel when someone snaps out or something.

Andrew: You show him where the gym is and all that.

Teacher: Yes, tell him what to do in gym, tell him what to do in music . . . Any other suggestions?

(Matthew continues with a subconversation of his own.)

Peter: Ask him if he likes to do it. Don't push him around or shove him around, yell at him. Like, if he's in the wrong spot, you don't say, ''Get out of there!''

Teacher: Yes, that might help.

Analysis. Some of the students' comments focused on presenting a positive image of the class to an outsider (Stage 3); they advocated prosocial courteous actions (Nicole, Peter, Andrew). Some engaged in Stage–2 role-taking when worrying about how Wayne might perceive their imperfections (John, Philip, Peter). Only Matthew refused to take part in this discussion. The comments made by the students indicated that there was a shared sense of community valuing, probably falling somewhere between Stages 2 and 3.

Anecdotal Records

Wayne was far more difficult than anyone had imagined he would be. He was under psychiatric care and swore that he had been told by the psychiatrist that he didn't have to listen to anyone but his mother and the psychiatrist. Because Wayne took this advice literally, he was absolutely impossible to deal with in the classroom. The very first day he joined Philip in taunting Andrew and in general insolent and disruptive behavior such as spitting at people, crawling into the closet, and pulling equipment out of the science box. As the days progressed, Wayne showed no improvement. He totally ignored any and all directions given him, turned on every student in the class (spitting and calling names), lighted matches in the bathroom and in the closet that housed the science chemicals, and when asked, judged his behavior to have been fairly good.

It took some days for everyone to extricate himself from association with Wayne. While the students were still in the throes of doing this, an interesting thing happened. The class split into "good kids" and "bad kids." John, Peter, Nicole, and Andrew remained aloof, unusually quiet, and conscientious in their schoolwork. John, Nicole, and Peter moved their desks together and rarely left each other's company. Philip and Thomas remained highly disruptive and resistant to control. Matthew was, as always, a person apart—identifying with no one and nothing except his dream of joining the U.S. Army.

Academic tension had not abated. On December 5 as the teacher was battling to teach fractions to a resistant math group, Nicole suddenly accused the school of failing to teach the students anything. She, John, and Andrew reported that Jude had told them that and that they believed him. The intensity of their attack on the school spurred the teacher to counter their arguments. A twenty-minute discussion ensued in which the teacher pointed out to them that despite her unrelenting efforts, only over their strongest opposition had she managed to teach them anything at all about fractions that day. They agreed. She then stated that their negative behavior was the biggest stumbling block to their learning.

Surprisingly, the pupils accepted this response. In fact, they then proceeded to support the teacher's statement by reciting a litany of their disruptive actions in their old schools which had prevented them from learning. The teacher then pointed up the high per-pupil cost to the taxpayer of special classes such as the one they were in. In a practical application of math, the group then calculated that the thirty-two adults who handled 150 students in Valley Brook would translate into five adults in the regular school. This impressed the class. Finally, the teacher commented that the past twenty minutes of discussion were supposed to have been applied toward the learning they so wanted to do. At this, the class sat in silent, sheepish agreement.

On December 6 the teacher took a sick day and stayed home. Philip was placed in another room; Thomas was placed one-on-one with the substitute; the assistant took the class. Upon the teacher's return, Philip made a conscious effort to create a good impression. For the first time in weeks he was well behaved.

December 12 was a turning point on two fronts. There was another terrible blow-up with Thomas in which he seemed on the verge of attacking the teacher with pointed scissors. The rest of the class were visibly shaken and united in fear for the teacher's safety. Most important, most unexpected, and most welcome, however, was Philip's capitulation on the level of his work. He came to this teacher and asked for his old books back—the ones that fit his instructional needs. Finally—after three months of school—Philip agreed to let the teacher teach him.

Things seemed much better for a few days. But on December 18 chaotic conditions returned—Philip angry, cursing, competitive; the class smashing their art projects; unruly behavior at math. The teacher called a special class meeting in which she called for group commitment:

December 18, Class Meeting

Teacher: In my opinion, this classroom is no longer a classroom. I'm calling this meeting because I want everyone's honest opinion and any suggestions. No one is to use anyone else's name so that the meeting won't deteriorate into name calling and the throwing of blame onto everyone else. I would like to open the floor and ask for perceptions—how other people see the classroom. Andrew?

Andrew: It's a disgrace.

John: This class is getting to be a *mess*!

Nicole: This classroom's a b . . i . . t . . no, I'll say it later.

Andrew: This classroom is getting to become the pits.

Peter: Because we're all going insane.

John: You're telling me.

Andrew: Only a few people here are in control.

The students' justification for their abominable behavior was not accepted by the teacher as legitimate:

Matthew: I know why I'm being bad. It's Christmas.

John: Everybody's starting trouble. I think I know why everybody's going off.

Teacher: Why?

John: Because it's Christmas.

Nicole: Even our bus driver said that, that we were real rowdy on the bus.

John: Everybody's so excited about Christmas.

Teacher: You blame it on *Christmas?* It's Christmas's fault, or the holiday's fault?

Nicole: Everybody's so happy about it.

Teacher: If you are happy about it, then why are you showing your happiness in such a destructive, horrible way?

Students: (Silence)

Teacher: You're not showing happiness. I see anger. I see disgust. I see no interest even in making Christmas presents.

Reminiscent of the October 13 meeting in which the teacher expressed her extreme discontent with Philip, she now expressed her discontent with her role in the class:

Teacher: I feel that I am holding up 99 percent of the classroom; that you count on me to hold it together . . . that you count on me to keep things going . . . that you count on me to teach you when you don't want to be taught . . . I feel that I have been expected to do everything in this classroom and that you do nothing. And the more I do, the worse you get.

Students: (Silence)

Teacher: Most of my time is spent making people sit down, making people pay attention, making people be quiet, making people do their work, taking it when people yell and scream and cuss at me when I tell them to do their work. And I'm telling you that I have come to the end of my rope. I can't do that any longer.

After some discussion in which the norm Separate the Deviant Member(s) from the Group was reproposed by one student, the teacher, striving for group unity, called for the group to make a commitment to itself:

Teacher: Well then, let me ask this question. Do you care about the classroom?

John, Peter, Nicole: Yes.

Matthew: Nope.

Andrew: I care.

Peter: It's like a family.

Nicole: I care about the classroom 'cause if, you know, we're going to hear it from the principal every day anyway.

Matthew: Yeah, she's a grouch.

Peter: I care about it cause, the people who snap out, I feel sorry for them. They have some mental problem.

John: If you don't got respect for yourself, you don't got respect for other people.

Analysis. The preceding comments showed a mixture of Stage 2 and Stage 3 community valuing. Peter clearly held a Stage–3 sense of community: (''It's like a family.'') Nicole described the community in Stage

2 terms—as a group of individuals who had to hold together to avoid a punitive principal. Matthew didn't value the community at all.

In addition, a norm of No Snapping Out was proposed here by Peter and discussed more in depth in the conversation that followed.

Issue. Near its end, the meeting moved to a different level of awareness. The discussion turned to one about high and low paths, the huge difference between the two, the true meaning of strength, and the necessary choice the group was being called upon to make:

Teacher: It's almost as if you think violence is cool.

Peter: I think it's sad.

Teacher: Where are your allegiances?

Student: What is that?

Teacher: What are you wedded to? What road are you going down? What path do you intend to follow?

John: A good one.

Teacher: I feel that the classroom is in real danger. And I feel that, if you have the strength, it would be wise to show it now.

John: I don't think some people got no strength in here. They just think that strength is for fighting.

Teacher: What do we mean when we do talk about strength?

John: Not this kind of strength.

Teacher: No, I don't mean that kind of strength.

John: And punching out people.

Teacher: No, that is not strength. That's weakness.

Peter: Insane strength.

Teacher: Sane strength. Sanity. Strength of sanity.

John: I don't even know what sanity is.

Peter: This kind of strength that we're all using . . .

Teacher: Right now.

Peter: Fighting is sad.

John: It's sad strength. Let's put it this way—it's sad.

Teacher: It's almost as if you're saying, "I can't be put anywhere. I won't make it in regular school. I'm no good. I'm a mess. What are you going to do about it?"

Student: I'm going to make it.

Teacher: I may *have* to divide the class, but I don't want to. I think the strength of our class is in staying together, but we're not staying together very well. . . . I am willing to make this classroom the best place that I can, but I have slowed up as of late because I don't feel that I'm getting any kind of feedback or any kind of help. I cannot care more about the classroom than you do because you make up the classroom; I don't. I have to take your lead, and if we have to run it like an armed camp to keep people down, then that's what we'll *have* to do, but I was hoping fervently that we wouldn't have to. It is up to you. It truly is up to you. I can only follow your lead.

Peter: Um hum.

Teacher: I can only teach you where you are. I've been walking around trying to teach you up here, finding that most of the class is down here.

Peter: I'm up there.

Teacher: There's a huge gap between the two.

Nicole: Peter's the only one I think who's been behaving.

Teacher: Now, I can either come down to where you are or I can ask you, which is what I'm doing, to come up and take what I have to give. I'm willing to teach. (Silence) But I cannot teach people who are not willing to learn.

John: You're telling me.

Analysis. The foregoing interchange shows the pupils at a fork in the road. They realize that they must choose between self-control and license, each with its accompanying results.

Outcome. The next morning Nicole, John, and Andrew came into the classroom saying that they had had a meeting on the bus that morning and had decided that Christmas was not a good excuse for acting as badly as they had. They had decided to improve. The days remaining before Christmas vacation were much more pleasant. It is hypothesized that these students were able to make the higher choice because of the Stage2/3 prerequisites developed during the fall months.

Anecdotal Records

On December 21 Thomas reported something he had not mentioned previously. This particularly quiet day he turned to this teacher and soberly told her that he "saw things"—animals, mostly. He said some of them didn't seem actual but were just imaginings, but that other times his visions came alive—the "things" were really there. Sometimes the things he saw (like green people and monsters) frightened him. At these times he was surprised that others didn't see them, too. Although this author did not say so to Thomas, she hypothesized that Thomas's basic vibratory rate had fallen to a level on which elementals from the lower astral planes exist, thereby exposing him to their presence and to their attentions—a condition known (in its extreme form) to medical science as "delirium tremens."

During this same period a bizarre episode with Matthew made the teacher acutely aware of the depths of his disturbance. At the end of a serene afternoon of making Christmas decorations and listening to Christmas music, Matthew turned suddenly from the tree he had been painstakingly—even lovingly—decorating, leaped from the table on which he had been standing, ran to an open jar of red paint, thrust one hand into the jar, and was stopped from smearing the paint on his face only by the alert reaction of the teacher. In a near-catatonic state Matthew allowed her to lead him to the sink and to clean his hand. Without a word he accepted his belongings, put on his coat, and left the room to get on his homebound bus.

Winter

Anecdotal Records

January was a marked improvement over December. The class had made the higher choice—to pursue self-control. Philip and Nicole, who had always been the most powerful group members, were now serving prosocial ends; and the class settled into a more harmonious routine. Philip, in particular, began to exercise his reasoning faculty in an effort to understand the prerequisites of positive social standing. The teacher had been reading to the class *The First Jungle Book* by Rudyard Kipling. The story is about a boy, Mowgli, who has been reared from infancy by wolves and other wild animals in an Indian jungle. Philip was particularly impressed with Mowgli's jungle training in right and wrong, and he reasoned that one must know such things before he can be trusted.

Interest in the moral-dilemma discussions increased markedly in January. Philip and Matthew participated with an interest and fervor which had been lacking before. The January 3 discussion was the first group activity since September in which Matthew remained focused and rational. Within a week he had written an excellent moral dilemma of his own (the first of several) with thoughtful probe questions; it elicited one of the best discussions to that date.

Matthew's Dilemma

Bill and Bob are friends. One day Bill and Bob went to buy a pack of cigarettes. They were fifty cents a pack. Bob picked up the cigarettes and put them in his pocket. He ran; so did Bill. Then, out came a security guard and caught Bill. He asked how old he was. Bill said fourteen. Bob made it home with the cigarettes. He wonders if he should tell his dad or mom or the security that he did it, not Bill. Should he tell and why?

Thomas, now seeing a psychologist and on medication, remained well balanced most of the month. The class was noticeably more tolerant of his occasional lapses (which were no longer violent) and remained quiet and unresponding during his outbursts. At these times he would return to normalcy much faster than he had before. On January 18 Thomas relinquished his cherished daily visit with the crisis-classroom teacher (who talked with him and gave him candy and iced tea) so that Nicole could go in his stead. He then suggested that the entire class should visit the crisis teacher on a rotating basis, with him taking a turn with the rest. Although this suggestion was not acted upon, Thomas had offered others what he had to give—a tremendous step forward for him.

The month was not unmarred by difficult days, but anecdotal records noted only three all month. One episode was precipitated by the teacher herself: because Philip, Nicole, and Andrew had been exhibiting such good behavior, the assistant bought them presents, which she gave to the teacher to distribute during a class meeting. The teacher did this despite her misgivings. At first the class was silent, but soon resentment began to spread. John pouted, Peter became openly insulting, Matthew began yelling at Wayne, and Thomas became defensive and angry. The present giving was a divisive influence.

Wayne was removed from Valley Brook on January 17 and placed in another setting for more-seriously disturbed children. His departure from the classroom was a relief to all.

During January small but significant daily occurrences were clear evidence of a budding Stage–3 community. The students chose to mingle socially during free moments of the day. No name calling or cutting remarks were heard by this teacher. For the first time all year, socializing required no outside control. They began to share personal problems with the group during Sharing Time. Interestingly, Philip, the leader in many respects, initiated this change. On January 18 he reported a problem he was having at home and discussed his feelings about it. The next day the teacher was having a private conversation with John about his fixity of behavior and the need for him to become more flexible before returning to regular school. The entire class gathered around to hear, and the private conversation turned into a group discussion about the need for all of them to begin altering the behaviors that would inhibit their success in a regular-school setting.

The academic atmosphere in the room had changed considerably. There was a sudden explosion of wanting to learn and to be taught. Instead of denying what they didn't know and blaming the school for poor instruction (as they had in the fall), the students had now accepted their limitations and were working to overcome them by changing themselves. Philip, Nicole, and John (all in the same math group) were particularly zealous. The January 17 entry in the teacher's anecdotal records reads

> Philip is bursting with energy to learn. He exceeds the group in English and revels in his superiority. He's doing all of his seatwork neatly and well. It's incredible. His math skills are moving: he *insists* on understanding every point and won't let the lesson stop until he has completely understood everything. Nicole, too, pushes in math; but she needs to write down every step on the board after me to get it into her head. John learns about as fast as Philip does.

A certain standard of behavior had developed among most of the class members; their toleration of aberrance had greatly diminished. On January 23, after several days of absence, Matthew (who had been acting particularly disturbed for the previous two weeks) returned to the room. As soon as he walked through the door, someone moaned, "Oh no," and someone else told him that the class had gone very well while he was gone. Matthew was visibly shaken, and for the remainder of the day he was emotionally high and disruptive. Thomas joined him, becoming loud, belligerent, and on the verge of explosion. Philip, Peter, John, Nicole, and Andrew retained their equilibrium.

The next day Matthew, the poorest athlete in the class, voluntarily removed himself from an important basketball game in gym. As he was coming off the court a student asked him if he was sick. "Yeah," he responded, "sick in the head." He assigned himself scorekeeper and remained on the sidelines keeping score and cheering his team on. Thus Matthew, too, gave what he had to give to the class.

(On January 25 Matthew was suspended from school for tying a rope around the neck of a younger child on his bus and then tying the rope around the same child's legs and pulling it as the child was trying to get off the bus. The class expressed its concern for Matthew in the January 26 Class Meeting.)

During January the subgroup of Nicole, John, and Peter became a cohesive Stage–3 unit. Although each was an integral part of the larger group, they enjoyed a particularly intimate friendship among themselves. The trio lovingly built a cozy study area in the back of the room using a table and construction paper, and occasionally they went there to talk. There had been no group discussion about the study area because its existence had not created any problems. Individuals had built such structures before without incident. Too, the teacher viewed the group's formation as healthy. However, on January 23, while the teacher was at lunch, the assistant "rewarded" the subgroup by giving them cookies. Although it was said that she intended to reward everyone, this was not made clear in her actions. Philip became uncontrollably violent, tore up the study area, and physically attacked Peter and John. This incident triggered an intense class meeting on January 26 in which the teacher forbade the formation of any special areas in or outside of the classroom. In addition, she put an end to the awarding of special privileges to anyone for any reason.

January 26, Class Meeting

Issue. Philip had attacked John and Peter for winning special privileges from the assistant. He had been sent to the crisis classroom for the afternoon and was, therefore, not present in the class meeting in which the issue of exclusion was discussed.

The subgroup exhibited a full understanding of Philip's motivation in destroying their study area:

Teacher: All right. I have a question now. Why do you think Philip reacted in that way?

John: 'Cause the assistant gave us cookies.

Peter: Yeah, and he's jealous 'cause we have that little thing there.

Nicole: And he can't be a part of it.

Teacher: I think that's the issue . . .

John: No, he said that he doesn't want to be a part of it.

Peter: No, you know he does. You *know* he does.

The teacher raised the problem of exclusion and met strong resistance from Nicole, Peter, and John:

Teacher: It seems to me that he is upset because you three have your own private place, and I think that's what we need to talk about.

Nicole: Oh no, we ain't getting rid of it!

Peter: No, we're not. I'm sorry.

Teacher: I'm not saying that we're getting rid of it. I'm saying this: if you're going to have it, it has to be open to everyone.

Nicole: No way!

Teacher: That area belongs to the classroom and therefore it belongs to everyone. You can't exclude anyone from being back there.

John: No! We're tearing it down.

Nicole: Three's company; four's a crowd.

Teacher: It *cannot* be exclusive.

Peter: Three's company; four's a crowd.

The teacher finally threatened to disband their study area if they didn't open it up to everyone.

Anaysis. In the foregoing interchange the teacher reproposed the norm The Group is One ("That area belongs to the classroom and therefore it belongs to everyone.'') Both she and the assistant had first proposed this norm in the November 3 Class Meeting when the group discussed the use of the class ball. Then and now the norm remained in the proposal phase. The stage of its proposal in January, however, was quite different from that in November.

In November the subgroup of Nicole, Peter, and John had not been definitively formed; by and large, the class was functioning as a group of separate individuals. In the November 3 Class Meeting, coming together into interest groups for mutual instrumental benefit (Stage 2) was in the proposal stage. Now, in January, Nicole, Peter, and John had firmly established a Stage–3 familial unit, which the teacher was asking them to extend to the entire class. Now in the proposal stage was The Group is One as a Stage–3 Community.

Outcome. Anecdotal records do not mention the study area again; evidently there were no further problems. The subgroup remained extremely close, and it wasn't until spring that The Group is One as a Stage–3 Community was realized.

Issue. Matthew's severe emotional problems had prevented him from becoming a full member of the class. As the rest of the students improved and began to form a sense of community, Matthew increasingly stood out as separate. In his absence the teacher brought him up as a topic of discussion:

Peter: What do we care about Matthew's future? That gets me. Why . . .

Teacher: Should we care? That's a good question.

Andrew: He's a member of the class.

Teacher: Should we care?

Nicole: Yes. Listen to this, people. He's one of the people of our class. We should care about him.

Student: He's a human being.

Nicole: And I knew Matthew for a very long time.

John: Amen!

Nicole: Two years. When I was at . . .

Teacher: (interrupting Nicole) I'm asking, should we care about it?

Student: Yes!

Teacher: Why?

Peter: Because he's a human being.

Teacher: And what does that mean?

Peter: And people care about human beings. People should care about human beings.

Teacher: All right. Let's try very hard to do the right thing by Matthew.

Analysis. The norm of Care is well established here (Phase 3, Stage 3 normative values and community valuing). Clearly, the students viewed the community as an entity which should care about and help its members. Too, the norm The Group is One in Care was supported (Phase 2) by Andrew and Nicole in Stage–3 language: "He's one of the people of our class. We should care about him." This exchange was in sharp contrast to the students' sentiments towards the plight of the teacher in the October 13 Class Meeting.

In the foregoing interchange the teacher interrupted Nicole because Nicole was preparing to reminisce about Matthew's, John's, and her experiences at the mental institution. Dwelling upon a past time in which these students had been at their most disturbed would have been counterproductive to their present growth.

Outcome. Despite the efforts of all class members to include and to help Matthew and despite Matthew's efforts to improve, Matthew's disturbance temporarily eclipsed his chances for successful classroom functioning; his days in this class were coming to an end.

Anecdotal Records

In February, school (now seen as a place of support) assumed a heightened importance in the students' lives. A general atmosphere of care reigned. Small actions by individuals showed that some change was taking place in them. Peter, for instance, who had always lived on the brink of destitution, found fifty cents lying on the shelf behind the teacher's desk. He turned it in. Andrew had befriended Matthew, who had moved his desk in with the rest of the class for the first time in months. They shared personal concerns; Matthew would accept Andrew's exhortations to improve his behavior, and made a visible effort to do so.

On February 14—Valentine's Day—a new child unexpectedly entered the class. His name was David. Full of apprehension because the last new child had been such a disaster and because David's records described him as "hopeless," this teacher waited for the problems to begin. They never did. David's nature was bright, positive, friendly, outgoing. He seemed to love the class and the class loved him. Nicole, John, and Peter opened their subgroup immediately and took him in. Whenever there was a disagreement in the group, David would always offer a positive solution. He smiled and laughed good naturedly at everything. He was a blessed ray of sunshine—a true valentine. This teacher reread his records and wondered if they had sent the wrong child. Only once did she witness a negative side to him, and her strong reaction stopped it for good. Until the end of the year David was a wonderful member of the class.

Although every effort was being made to work with Matthew, his disturbance was too severe. On February 27 he was suspended from his bus—for what, the teacher was not then told. On that day he reverted to his former intensely disturbed behaviors. Anecdotal records read: "He wrote curse words and obscene phrases all over his desk, which I made him clean off. His schoolwork was practically illegible; what he did do was wrong, and he wouldn't correct anything unless I stood over him every second. He was so flighty, I moved his desk to the back of the room again; and it looks like we're back to where we started."

Matthew wrote a story, "Hot Rod," which he asked the teacher to read several times. She hadn't the time then, so she told him to put it on her desk. In retrospect she realized the significance of this story.

Hot Rod

One day in the year 2000 Matthew, age twenty, joined the U.S.A. Army. Now, at 2004 he is in the Army. He had a mission—to run twenty miles to Apollo, a small city. On the way, about six miles, he stopped at a hotel at Wikinsburg. Here he thought he was going to get some rest, but a German spy overheard him talking on the phone saying that he was on a secret mission and he must stop it. So he planted a time bomb at the bottom of the building. Later—BOOM! The bomb blew up. The building was on fire. All the people got out. They were all quiet when a lady yelled out, "My son Rob is in there!" Matthew asked her what house. She said, "On the twentieth floor—house nine." Matthew went into the fire. When he got to the tenth floor, when two feet away, the roof fell in. Now he can't get out!

On March 1, the teacher learned the reason for Matthew's suspension. He had put his hands down the pants of the same child he had roped on January 25. The boy's father, who had accepted Matthew's previous aggression towards his son, was furious at this and demanded that Matthew be removed from the bus and the school. The father decided to press charges but then reconsidered. The county juvenile center however, which had dealt with Matthew before, urged him to proceed with the legal action. He did so; Matthew was immediately removed from the school and eventually placed back into the state mental institution as a day student.

March events had a great effect on the class. The most cathartic was a confrontation between Thomas and the teacher on March 5. On that day Thomas and Andrew were having a mild disagreement about the best make of car. Thomas claimed the 1979 Chevrolets had not been released yet. David, who was listening to the conversation and who knew a lot about cars, pleasantly corrected Thomas: 1979 Chevrolets *had* been released. Thomas turned to David and viciously told him to shut up or he'd punch David's face in. The teacher intervened immediately, telling Thomas he could not threaten anyone in the room. Thomas argued with her, saying he could do anything he wanted and that, if she didn't shut up he was going to punch her in the face to shut her up. He then got up, stalked the room like an animal, and left.

The principal had been sent for in the middle of this confrontation, but she was in a meeting which she did not leave. Later, when the teacher related the incident to her, the principal answered, "Well, I hope you'll give him a good fight if he does hit you." This was an odd and frightening remark, since even the male teachers in the building had announced in September that Thomas was too strong and violent for them to handle. Now, in March, he was much larger and stronger than he had been in September. No overt action was taken by the teacher at this time, but the seeds of her changed approach towards Thomas were planted.

The subgroup of Nicole, John, Peter, and now David was flowering. They played independently of adult direction on the baseball field, settling differences among themselves. This teacher was fortunate to witness one instance of in-group control: John became angry because Peter had failed to "sink out" far enough in the field to catch Nicole's hit. John began to cry and ran to this teacher to complain. Peter and David promptly threw themselves to the ground and mocked a tantrum—feet kicking, fists pounding, wails emitting from their mouths. It was perfect. John sheepishly returned to his group.

Nicole led the four in baseball and would take on all three of the boys and beat them. They may have made strange companions, but they did provide each other with a strong sense of belonging. An anecdotal entry reads: "When we were walking back to the school (from a playing field) another teacher asked me if we'd been somewhere special—they looked so happy and full of camaraderie.''

Into this cohesive foursome entered Philip with Thomas one day at recess. The subgroup welcomed Philip but summarily rejected Thomas. Reportedly, Peter referred to Thomas's race as their reason for not wanting to include him. Philip promptly knocked Peter down and called them all prejudiced. The class was brought in. The issue was then discussed in the March 16 Class Meeting and a group policy was formed.

March 16, Class Meeting

Issue. Philip and Thomas tried to enter a baseball game Nicole, Peter, John, and David were playing. Thomas was not accepted by the four. The reasons for their rejection of him were debatable. Philip claimed they were racial; Nicole, David, and John insisted it was Thomas's violence that frightened them:

Peter: I said you didn't want him to play because he was black.

Nicole: No, no, no, no. It's because he takes bad tempers and I know how many times John hit me with that ball.

David: 'Cause if Thomas got hit with the ball, he would have took a snap out, and probably killed John.

Thomas: Why should you let Philip play and won't let me play?

Nicole: Cause you take a snap-out, Tom. It's not for racial reasons. That's what I got to say. It isn't for no racial reasons.

John: I don't feel like getting killed.

Nicole: Because John has hit me in the head, in the back, the legs, and the ear with that hard ball.

Analysis. The subgroup of Nicole, Peter, David, and John reiterated the norm of No Snapping Out, which had been proposed and discussed at the December 18 Class Meeting. Now they were arguing at Stage 3 for its being upheld: all were genuinely concerned with the physical well-being of their classmates. Because the group so readily agreed and acted upon this reason for excluding Thomas, the norm was operating at Phase 3 within their group. Philip, however, seemed to have acted on the norm

The Group is One when he tried to bring Thomas with him into the playing group, although he verbally offered no support for this hypothesis.

Outcome. After some discussion in which everyone, including Thomas, participated, the following group policy was voted upon and unanimously accepted: The baseball games were open for anyone and everyone in the classroom. The first time someone seriously snapped out, that person was to be barred from the lunch-time baseball games for one week.

There were no more problems with Thomas's joining the baseball games. He rarely joined them, but when he did, he controlled his temper.

Anecdotal Records

In retrospect, the Thomas incident and the subsequent playing policy, which officially opened the games to everyone, were the beginning of the end for the subgroup of Nicole, John, Peter, and David. The subgroup did not fade away quickly or easily, however. The March 30 Class Meeting was ample evidence of that.

A major policy shift occurred on March 15. It had become increasingly clear to the teacher that the classroom atmosphere had far surpassed that of the students' environments outside of the schoolroom. The sharing of their negative out-of-school realities during Sharing Time was in conflict with the positive reality everyone had worked so hard to create in the room. Therefore, at the assistant's suggestion, the teacher eliminated Sharing Time and had the class memorize and discuss famous quotations and meaningful poetry about high and positive ways to approach life. By reciting these quotations and poems from memory, they could earn bonus points. These materials had previously been used only incidentally in the program.

The class was making visible gains and other faculty members were noticing. Some complimented the class; others reacted negatively. Now that the students had achieved some measure of self-control, they became acutely aware of their own power. Their sense of justice was strong and they began to apply classroom standards to those with whom they came into contact, including the adults in the school. Needless to say, this created problems.

March 23, Class Meeting

Issue. The class's improvement in behavior had been noticed by other faculty members. The gym teacher had complimented the teacher on their improvement and the teacher reported the compliment to a delighted group in this meeting.

Teacher: I have a report to give to the class. The gym teacher stopped me the other day and he said, "What's the matter with your class?" I said, "What do you mean, what's the matter with my class?" He said, "They've been so together."

Philip: Yep.

John: I thought you were going to start yelling at us (very pleased, laughing with pleasure). I thought you were going to say something bad about us. I was going to say, "What's the matter with our class? What the *heck's* the matter with our class?"

Teacher: A couple of other teachers definitely have looked at me as if they agree—that they can't believe it either.

Assistant: Well, I've noticed myself that, you know, general talk going around. The gym teacher was in the lunchroom today—he watched. The principal—everytime I looked up, eyes were on our table, and I was really very proud that you guys were sitting there. They were having nice conversations; they weren't screaming or yelling or anything. And I am really proud of the behavior.

One other faculty member (an assistant in another classroom) had not reacted positively, and one student complained about what he judged to be her unfair treatment of him at lunch. This class's assistant encouraged the student to accommodate himself to the less-than-desirable behavior of that adult. The teacher then tried to focus the group's attention on the positive results of its behavior change:

John: Well, I just had my straw up like this like blowing through it and she starts jumping all over my case. I don't think that is fair, man. And she said I . . .

Assistant: Do not say anything. Do not say anything.

John: I didn't say anything. I just started screaming back at her.

Assistant: Well, that's exactly what I mean.

Philip: John, you ain't allowed to scream back at the teacher.

Teacher: I think all-in-all that the class has most definitely improved and that the rest of the school doesn't know what to think about it.

That's why everyone's looking so closely because I don't think any-
body believes it! And even myself, I'm sort of like . . . wait a
minute, let's see how long this lasts. But it has lasted for a long
time, and I hope this is a permanent change and we can continue.

Analysis. Clearly, the class valued its prosocial image. Although few
students spoke during this interchange, John and Philip presumably represented the other students' feeling in their remarks. Together with the
teacher's and the assistant's reports, there seemed to be a Stage–3 sense
of community valuing operating at this time.

Anecdotal Records

March ended with the acquisition of a new student—Charles—who
had been switched from another classroom in the building. The students
were thrilled to have him because he was an excellent athlete. He, Philip,
and Andrew united on the basketball court where their superior playing
skill dazzled all who watched them. This new subgroup (which had
consisted of only Andrew and Philip before) was grounded in competitive
skill building. The three were close enough to each other in ability to
push each other to the limit during daily, deadly serious practice sessions.
Soon, some adult male teachers from the other school were joining these
thirteen-year-olds on the court.

The last of March also dealt a final blow to the power of Jude, the
bus driver. On March 30, Philip and Andrew burst into heated argument
about something Jude had said to them on the bus. The teacher was
stunned at its suddenness and its intensity. The root of the anger lay in
Jude's claim that he was a good friend of the principal and that he had
control over their next-year's school placements.

The teacher was forced to let the argument continue for a while;
finally, however, it cooled down enough for her to say something she
felt they needed to know: Jude had had a history of "adopting" handsome boys who rode his bus and of taking these boys off on weekend
trips. Philip had gone with him several times; one of those times even
his parents hadn't known where he was staying. No one in the class ever
knew what happened on those trips because Philip had been sworn to
secrecy. This day the teacher talked about homosexuals, their tastes,
their habits, and their preference for young, handsome boys. Nicole
mentioned the Gacey murders (sensational homosexual killings of young
boys in Chicago).

Although the teacher was careful to deny a student's statement that
she was calling Jude a homosexual, the necessary impact was made on
the students. To protect herself and the school from a possible backlash,
the teacher submitted a written report to the principal detailing what had

been said. This discussion with the students created difficulties for the teacher (see spring anecdotal records). After the discussion, however, the pupils' attitude toward Jude became noticeably cooler. He quit his job on May 1.

March 30, Class Meeting

Issue. The issue of name calling resurfaced. The students openly reported the violators and expressed their disapproval. Philip then proposed, and the students unanimously accepted, a group name-calling policy which was quite stringent.

Philip: I move that the person that's calling somebody names should lose points and the person who's being called names, if he don't ignore it, he also loses points.

David: I agree.

Nicole: All in favor say aye.

Students: Aye.

Nicole: All opposed say nay.

Students: (Silence)

Analysis. The No-Name-Calling norm, last addressed in the fall in the November 15 and December 1 Class Meetings, was here further strengthened. On November 15 the students voted to ignore name calling. On December 1 they decided to delete points from the name caller. Now, on March 30, they voted to delete points from both the name caller and the person who was called the name if he did not ignore it. Clearly, the class wanted once and for all to put an end to this activity. The original No-Name-Calling norm was at Phase 6b at this meeting: students reported violations publicly. The elaborated version of the norm voted on at this meeting was at Phase 3: the students expected it to be upheld.

Outcome. The No-Name-Calling policy was violated within a week, with cathartic consequences.

Issue. Nicole had been talking back to faculty members when she felt they were mistaken in judgment. Her responses had been extremely insolent and she was difficult to deal with in this class meeting. The root of the problem lay in larger classes wanting to take a playing field from the small subgroup of Nicole, Peter, John, and David. The subgroup realized that it could not in fairness claim the large playing field if a larger class came along. The teacher then proposed that the entire class play together outside, so that they could hold the bigger field. John liked the idea, but Nicole (whose power within her subgroup would have been threatened with the addition of Philip, Charles, and Andrew) *vehemently* opposed it:

Teacher: Have we already talked about what we're going to do about the baseball?

Nicole: Yes. If any other class comes along and they want to play, we got to go to the little field, because there's only four of us and there's ten of them.

Teacher: Unless the whole class decides to play. Then you have a right to a big field.

Nicole: No way!

John: Can we vote on that? Can we vote on one day, the class plays together?

Nicole: No!

Teacher: Certainly.

Nicole: I am not going to vote!

Teacher: That's your right. You lose the power (of vote).

(General commotion)

Teacher: Put the motion on the floor, John. We're allowed to vote on it. Now, if you're going to defeat it, you can defeat it, but . . .

Nicole: (Yelling and pounding on the table) *O.K. Defeat it!!!*

Teacher: We have a right to vote on it!

Assistant: *I* make the motion. I move that we divide our time up and let the class play as a whole. One day basketball.

Philip: Nope.

Assistant: Or, two days basketball.

David: No.

Outcome. Playing as a class during lunch recess was defeated.

Analysis. Once again, the norm being proposed by the adults and supported by John was the Group is One. This norm was last in evidence
at the January 26 Class Meeting when the class expressed its concern for
Matthew in Phase–3, Stage–3 language and when the subgroup of Peter,
Nicole, and John fought to maintain an exclusive study area (thereby
holding the norm at Phase 1). Here, applied to another issue (outside
ball games), the norm is at proposal Phase 1 once again.

Spring

Anecdotal Records
    Thomas had in many ways become separated from classroom activ-
ities during the month of March. He worked in isolation. The teacher
had written a detailed report on his year's behavior, had shown it to him,
and had promised to give it to the head of his home if he threatened
anyone again. Thomas valued the head of the home's opinion of him
and his fear that the teacher might show a most-disparaging report to the
head had kept him under reasonable control throughout most of March.
    By the end of the month, however, he had begun to show small signs
of returning to his former belligerent self. Starting with speaking nastily
to the assistant, his insolence began to spread to other areas. For three
consecutive gym days, the gym teacher noted, Thomas had been increasingly surly and unwilling to participate in the gym skill-building activities. On April 2 Thomas refused to participate in the exercises at all.
This teacher reprimanded Thomas with venom and told him to leave if
he was not willing to participate; the door was open and he was more
than free to go through it. Thomas left.
    The teacher, assuming Thomas had gone to the crisis classroom,
waited until gym was over to report the episode to the principal. It was
then discovered that Thomas had left the building and had gone to a
friend's house in the neighboring city (his original home). His exit,
although not permanent, was a relief to this teacher; but the administration was naturally upset.
    The next day at lunch the class engaged in a name-calling battle

initiated by a child from another classroom (breaking their new rule about ignoring name calling). As punishment, the principal ordered them to sit apart from the rest of the school, although absolutely no action was taken against the student from the other class who had started the name calling. The group had an emergency class meeting in which the students accepted the punishment as fair:

April 3, Special Class Meeting

Teacher: How do you feel about this move? Do you think that it is justified?

David: Our actions in the front of the room may give a bad impression for Valley Brook.

Peter: I think it's right. It's teaching us a lesson.

John: Not me, cause I didn't do anything.

Nicole: Well, still, John.

Peter: I do, because everybody calls people names, so I think it's right.

Philip: Well, the kid started with me. I didn't start it with the kid.

David: I know . . .

Teacher: Peter says that, in a way, it will teach us a lesson if we move.

David: And I say, yes, it will teach us a lesson.

Teacher: And David says it will teach us a lesson. John says he wishes we didn't have to.

Peter: Let's have a vote on whether it teaches us a lesson or it doesn't teach us a lesson.

David: Why? It's no use. We're going to move whether we vote yes or no.

John: I know.

Teacher: I just think it's a shame that after all the distance we've traveled all year that we just end up being put in the back of the room.

Student: (Mock crying): We're babies.

David: We made a boo-boo. . . .

John: I wonder what the other school will say?

Analysis. This exchange contained Stage–3 reasons for accepting the punishment as fair: concern with making a good impression (David, John) and the group's acceptance of its responsibility for the actions of fellow class members (Nicole, Peter, David). John did not want to accept the punishment on the basis of *his* not having done anything wrong (Stage 2), and Philip offered a Stage–2 defensive justification for his having called the student from the other class a name. Overall, however, the class seemed to share a Stage–3 sense of community. Notable was the group's sense of powerlessness to influence the decision of the principal ("It's no use. We're going to move whether we vote yes or no"); the democratic atmosphere that prevailed in the classroom did not extend beyond its confines.

The norms The Group is One and No Name Calling were also active at this meeting. The students expected that all should and would accept responsibility for their actions (Stage 3, Phase 3); Peter and David expressed their disapproval of the group's violation of its No-Name-Calling policy (Phase 5).

Outcome. This punishment turned into a powerful impetus for group unity (see succeeding anecdotal records).

Anecdotal Records

On April 4 the principal informed the teacher of her deep displeasure. The expulsion of Thomas from the gym class and the conversation with the class about Jude, the bus driver, were the reasons for her anger. Also, the teacher had submitted to the principal a copy of the report on Thomas, with a request that he be removed from her class. The principal stated that she and one of her superiors had found the teacher's fear of Thomas's violence amusing: a mere threat to strike a teacher was no basis for removal of a pupil from a room. Finally, the principal stated that she was thinking of putting those students who were to leave Valley Brook the following year (because of their advanced ages) into institutional or juvenile-delinquent settings.

That day at lunch the principal stiffened her punishment of the class.

The class had taken seats separated from the rest of the school by two or three empty lunch tables. Everyone had acted well and was pleased with the situation. But as they were getting ready to leave, the principal angrily informed them that they were to sit at a table at the farthest end of the lunchroom (with about ten empty tables between the class and the rest of the school) and that everyone was to sit in a single line facing the wall. At this, the class began to react. Andrew, in particular, expressed a deeply felt sense of injustice and said repeatedly, "This is unnecessary. I said, this is unnecessary." The group complied, but it was clearly traumatized by this edict.

This teacher, who witnessed the incident, stressed to the class the importance of finding something good in the situation. David was the first to do so. The class was to face a colorful mural which David praised. Soon, several others followed his lead. From this day forward the teacher gave up her lunch break and ate with the class. The assistant brought in a daily centerpiece—flowers, etc.—and both adults sat on the other side of the table and carried on a conversation with the students.

During this trying period the class read Rudyard Kipling's poem "If" daily and drew great strength from it. The teacher repeatedly stressed the importance of getting the good from a difficult situation; of blessing those who have wronged you; of maintaining inner peace, strength, and equilibrium in the midst of outer storm; and of drawing together and nurturing the group's good.

The afternoon of April 4, during art, the entire group visibly pulled together into a Stage–3 caring unit. The class was weaving Easter baskets. David ran around busily helping people finish. Nicole wove three or four extras to give to anyone who couldn't finish his on time.

Although the separation from the school was a powerful impetus for class unity, the group had made significant progress even before this challenge. The librarian in the other school (who saw every class weekly) merged a second class with this teacher's because, she told the second teacher, this teacher's group was the only one in Valley Brook that knew what it was doing, was self-directed, and could, therefore, merge successfully with another group of students—which it did.

Meanwhile, this teacher, remembering the principal's threat to institutionalize those students slated to leave Valley Brook, took quick and vigorous action. The next week was Easter vacation. Through personal contacts in another school district she obtained Metropolitan Achievement Tests (Valley Brook had discontinued all standardized testing). For the next week she put the students through hours of testing. In addition, she had them write essays about (1) their behavior (whether they thought they were ready to return to a regular school program and why; how they had changed this year from last) and (2) their feelings about the class meetings and dilemma discussions (see Appendix C). The teacher then spent her nights scoring achievement tests and putting together a package in which each student's academic and behavioral growth from September to April was assessed. At the end of April, this package was submitted to the principal along with a copy of this teacher's acceptance letter into the doctoral program of the Harvard Graduate School of Education.

As previously stated, the punitive isolation of the class in the lunchroom merged the class into one cohesive unit. Most days everyone played baseball together on the large playing field. Even Thomas joined them. One lunch time the teacher held David and Charles in at the lunch table because they were giggling and joking. She told the rest of the class they could go out and play. Philip and Andrew (who had opted to play basketball that day) left; but Nicole, John, and Peter stood by the table— bats, balls, and gloves in hand—and waited. When the teacher told them again that they were free to go, Nicole answered, "No, we're a team." At this reminder David and Charles settled down immediately; all of them were then able to leave together.

At the end of that same day, the class, except for Andrew (who shot baskets alone) and David (who stayed in the room with the teacher as punishment for something unrecorded) went out to play baseball. As the class played, David sat on the window ledge inside the room and animatedly watched the game from there. He bolted out to meet the group at the end of the game and walked with them to their buses on the other side of the school. The teacher watched the students stroll across the playing fields completely controlled, easily interacting with each other, looking like any group of normal thirteen-year-olds, and she felt satisfied.

The class had become a group to notice—not only by students and teachers in Valley Brook, but by people in the other school. Everyone in the class commented on its fish-bowl existence and John voiced what may have been a group sentiment: "Yeah, they are [looking at us], but I wonder why? Us?!"

On April 20 the principal offered the class its former lunch table back. To her visible surprise, everyone immediately said "No." Later, at the class meeting, a formal vote was taken on the issue. The negative verdict stood.

April 20, Class Meeting

Issue. The class discussed and voted upon whether it would accept the principal's offer to return to its former eating table.

John: He'll go "bald eagle" or somebody will get called names. That's why I don't want to go back. And then we might have to go back and then we might really get in trouble.

Nicole: My suggestion.

John: And we'll never get out of it.

Philip: I want to stay back there because I don't like it up in front.

Teacher: What don't you like?

Philip: Too much noise.

John: And you can't even talk. You can't even hear yourself talk.

Philip: And Earl, every time he talks, you can hear him across the cafeteria.

Peter: And Mark. . . .

Nicole: If we start, like . . . If the principal sees the assistant hollering at us, then we're going to have a black point against us.

John: And if we do go back there it'll be so noisy you can't hear yourself talking to other people. Then, if you yell, the assistant will yell at you, and then that's another black point against us.

The group is confident of its ability to return to the former trying eating situation and makes it clear that its decision not to do so is purely a matter of personal preference and not of fear of losing control:

Philip: I think we can go back, though.

David: I don't want to go back. We're capable of going back, but we don't want to.

Charles: We're capable.

Analysis. This interchange was Stage–2 in so far as it focused upon instrumental avoidance of punishment (John, Nicole). It was Stage 3 in so far as it (1) rejected outsiders' behavior because it did not live up to this group's standards (Philip, John, Peter) and (2) valued the maintenance of a positive group image (Nicole, John).

The norm The Group is One appeared to have been operating here and at Stage 3, Phase 3. The students expressed an awareness of their collective strength when they judged themselves capable of returning to a difficult eating situation with no further incident and of their power to make and to stand by a collective decision.

Outcome. Everyone but Andrew (who stated that he wanted to return to the former eating table) voted to remain in the back of the cafeteria.

Issue. The students and teacher had been discussing and preparing for the students' return to the regular school. The teacher never told the class of the principal's threat either to institutionalize them or to place them in juvenile-delinquent special-school settings. However, she did exhort them to act normally. Philip guessed the danger the class was in during this meeting:

Teacher: Now there are some things we have to think about here. By choosing to stay in the back we may make the principal slightly angry. She might be a little angry because we are not accepting her offer. Now that means that if we ever *do* want to go back to the front table, she may say "No"; so we have to be prepared now to make this table our own, and that also means that we have to be prepared to act normally.

Philip: I got a good point. What if she stays mad, like you know, at the end of the year when it's time for us to go back to regular school? Will this go against us? Do you think she'll do that?

Teacher: Well, I don't think she'll do that. Plus the fact, Phil, that I have your test scores. I have the things that you've written; but most of all, I have your behavior. And as long as I have your behavior, I can fight down to the wire. No, I don't think she'll be able to get you in that way, *especially* if you hold on to your behavior.

Assistant: You're getting the opportunity *now* to show that your behavior has improved and that you do know how to behave.

Anecdotal Records

Thomas became unusually cooperative during April. The teacher had stopped trying to interact with him personally. He was assigned daily folder work (which was corrected and returned to him) but was given no direct instruction. In addition, the teacher had assumed and maintained a hard and uncompromising stance towards any show of negativity from him. The minute he began to speak or act in a questionable manner she would verbally attack him with such force that he would stop it immediately. From this unrelenting repression of his lower side, a much nicer side of Thomas emerged.

April 27, Class Meeting

Issue. The teacher had received information about Matthew's progress as a day student at the state mental hospital. She shared her information with the class:

Teacher: I got a report from a fairly first-hand source—from someone who used to work at the state hospital and who knows some people who are working there now. Evidently, Matthew is now in a day program and not an in-patient. He goes to school there during the day. They told her that Matthew is the *best* pupil in his class, and that, not only is he good academically, but he's getting up in class and telling the kids what to do and what not to do—what's good and what's bad . . .

John: What!

Teacher: And he's telling them, Matthew's . . .

Student: Matthew?

Andrew: Is that the *real* Matthew?

Teacher: And he's telling them that, if they don't straighten up, they're never going to make it in the regular world. She said that he's just the model student.

John: (Happily laughing)

Thomas: Matthew!? Who used to be in *this* classroom?

Teacher: So we had an effect on Matthew.

John: This classroom's Matthew?

Teacher: Yes.

John: . . . The crazy Matthew? The jokey Matthew?

Teacher: The Matthew we had here. All of our discussions and our talking evidently had some effect.

Thomas: How did he . . .?

John: That's what I'm trying to figure out. How could he *do* that?

Andrew: I don't believe it. He acts so good up at the state hospital and when he gets down here, he's the devil.

Teacher: You know what? When Matthew was at the state hospital before, they said he was terrible—that he was their "worst." When he went back this year, the psychiatrist said he had never seen him so good—that Matthew was really open to discussion. He talked about his feelings; he talked about things. . . . I thought he was getting better, too. He *was* getting better. And now they say he's the best student in class.

John: They must have brainwashed him. They had to have brainwashed him.

Teacher: No, it was from here, John.

David: We calmed him down.

John: I can't believe it.

David: Open discussion calms you down.

Teacher: It does. It makes you see the sense of things in a lot of ways. Well, enough about that.

Analysis. The teacher (and later David) attributed Matthew's change to the power of the classroom, in particular to the open discussions and class meetings. John, Thomas, and Andrew didn't sense this connection and spent their time marvelling at the "miraculous" change.

Issue. With the exception of Andrew (and often Thomas), the class had been playing baseball together during lunch recess. Andrew would join them occasionally (something he never did during fall and winter), but his passion for excellence in basketball kept him on the basketball court most days. Philip and Charles would join Andrew on the court, but they also spent a great deal of time playing baseball with Nicole, John, Peter, and David.

In this class meeting the assistant exhorted every class member to play baseball regularly (and without their daily squabbles):

Assistant: I think that if we are going to play this game of baseball, *everybody* plays. Why not? Thomas has played a few times last week and he enjoyed it. And he played well. So, I see no reason why the class should not play as a whole and play harmoniously together.

The students were amenable to this suggestion, but they expressed concern that Nicole, who owned most of the baseball equipment, would exercise her ownership rights to control the game. It was decided that the teacher should either buy baseball equipment or bring in personal equipment for the class to use. She did the latter.

The class also formulated and unanimously accepted playing rules. Following is an example of the process of the first rule's formulation:

Teacher: The next thing we have to decide upon is how sides are going to be picked.

Philip: All right . . . Say there's three people who want to be captain; two of them flip a coin; whoever wins that; and then the other . . . Or, they pick numbers.

Thomas: Nope, if there's three, right?—Those two should go, and whoever wins that . . .

John: No, pick out of a hat.

Philip: Pick names out of a hat . . .

Teacher: Captains shall be chosen by picking names out of a hat or other container. How about this: the first name picked will get the first choice?

Andrew (and other students):.: Yes.

John: And the second one gets first up.

Thomas: Yeah!

Teacher: All right. We have proposed that captains shall be chosen by picking two names from a hat or other container, *before* lunch. The first name picked gets the first pick of players, and the second name picked gets the first up.

Philip: How many people agree? Say "aye."

Students: Aye.

Philip: All opposed say "nay."

Students: (Silence)

Philip: It's passed.

Similarly, three more rules were constructed. By the end of the meeting, the class had instated four baseball rules which held until the end of the year:

1.   All baseball members must agree to play baseball before we go to lunch. Anyone who wants to join the game after it has begun will not be allowed to play.
2.   Captains shall be chosen by picking names out of a hat or other container. The first name picked will get the first choice. The second one gets the first up.
3.   In order for our class to keep the large baseball field when a larger class wants it, we must have six players. In order for our class to keep the small baseball field when a larger class wants it, we must have four players.
4.   In order for our class to play whiffle ball on the macadam when a larger class wants it, we must have six players.

Analysis. The norm The Group is One (On the Playing Field) was solidly in evidence at this meeting (Stage 3, Phase 2). The class easily accepted the idea of playing as a team; to that end, it solved the problem of equipment ownership and established excellent baseball rules.

If the reader will recall, on November 3 the teacher had tried to get the group to say it wanted to share the classroom equipment, and the assistant first proposed that the class should play as a group on the baseball field. A system of sharing the ball was voted upon, but it was never instituted in reality; until April the students steadfastly refused to play ball as a whole class. Clearly, they had traveled a great distance forward.

Anectodal Records

At the end of April, the teacher told the class that she would be returning to Harvard the next year and that it was time for all of them to start preparing for the next year, too. At first the students showed no particular reaction, but soon the days grew more tense and some of their old disturbed behaviors reemerged. An excerpt of the anecdotal record of that time reads:

> I can't tell if we're going forwards or backwards or both at once. On the one hand their gains have been great; and for several—perhaps all—I feel they may be permanent. Yet, I still see croppings of their old insecurities and mine, since we are mirrored in each other. I wonder what they're thinking—how they are assimilating the changes.

Several students began to voice fears about returning to the regular school system. In response to this, the teacher changed the academic program to approximate the regular-school program. They were given English and vocabulary tests which were graded (in violation of the school policy of no grades); they learned how to outline a chapter; they were expected to attend to the lesson steadily and without incident for a full class period. The students enjoyed this change in atmosphere and it was maintained until the end of the year.

The next-year-placement decisions took place in May. Peter and David were to remain in Valley Brook, because the 1978–1979 year had been their first there and school policy dictated keeping most students for two years. Peter was disappointed but was heartened by the news that the teacher had requested his and David's placement in an excellent class situation for the next year. This teacher's recommendations that Philip, Nicole, Andrew, and John be returned to a regular eighth grade with resource-room help as needed were accepted carte blanche by the principal, who now made no effort to interfere in the running of the classroom. The regular-school-district placement officers remembered Philip, Nicole, Andrew, and John as they had been before and were most reluctant to accept them back into the school systems. However, the teacher's reports and the students' testifying for themselves during the placement meetings changed the placement officers' minds. All recommended students were accepted back into their home school districts.

The reaction from these four students was one of anxiety. Compounding the problem was the reluctance on the part of several of their parents to support their reentry into a regular-class setting. This year had, in many respects, been the only successful year of their school histories. John's parents didn't want him returned at all, and John had to argue for days to convince them he was ready. (They later told this teacher that John's closely reasoned arguments in his own behalf had persuaded them that he was, indeed, mature enough to return.) Nicole's parents also opposed her return to regular school and refused to show any support for her reentry. It was only Philip's and Andrew's parents who strongly supported their sons' return to the regular-school system.

Although she was receiving no support from home, Nicole had been making a visible effort to prepare herself for a change in status. Returning to regular-class placement meant conforming to the social expectations of the other eighth-grade girls: Nicole had let her hair grow out of a tomboy cut at the teacher's prompting. Near the end of April and into May she made a much greater effort to feminize herself. She curled her hair with an electric curling iron daily (bringing the iron into the classroom for "touch-ups"), and wore pink nail polish and an Avon necklace. The boys encouraged her activities; Peter wrote her poetry:

> Roses are red,
> Violets are blue,
> Beginning to be a girl
> Won't make an ape out of you!

The principal tried to return Thomas to regular-class placement. The representative was wary of her recommendation and rejected it outright when he read this teacher's report on Thomas's behavior.

The class had been handling Thomas well. The teacher kept him reined in by not allowing him outside of the confines of the group. In the classroom he was under the strictest, yet kindest, control; on the playground he was required either to play with the class in a group game or to sit quietly and watch Andrew and whoever was with Andrew shoot baskets. If he didn't want to do that, he had to stay inside with the teacher. Roaming the playground alone (where he would attack other students) or pairing with anyone outside of this class was forbidden. This tight rein kept Thomas peacefully restrained.

The group was more cohesive than ever. They started scheduling baseball games with a well-behaved and athletically competent learning-disabled class for lunch and for end-of-the-day recess, and then announcing their schedule to this teacher. The excellent thing about these games was the students' ability to monitor themselves. All differences were settled strictly by the rules of baseball. The other class, which was accustomed to allowing exceptions and "letting people slide," had to adjust rather abruptly to this class's insistence on adhering to the rules impartially. The other class loved it, however, because they altered their usual recess break and worked an extra forty-five minutes on academics in order to meet this teacher's class at the end of the academic day.

May 11, Class Meeting

Issue. The class had signed up to go on its first trip—to the zoo. The teacher feared to let the class go off on its own and explained her reasons at this meeting. The students, however, insisted that they were old enough, sane enough, and responsible enough to spend the day unsupervised.

Philip: Can't we, like when we get there, can't we make up a place to meet? Say, if we want to go somewhere and you tell us to meet in a certain place for lunch. Can we do that?

Teacher: The answer is "No," and let me tell you why.

David: We're not apes.

Students: (Laughter)

David: We're not apes.

Peter: We're not going to go out in the cages . . .

John: We're going to have to be trusted in regular school, so why can't you trust us now?

Teacher: In this classroom and outside, I am impressed with how well the class controls itself. We've come a long way, and I trust you to a great extent. However, when it comes to going to the zoo, that means that we are going to be mixing with a lot of other classes in this building—with kids that are not well together. I know from experience that when you get around someone who is out of control, you tend to lose it yourselves. And it would be the worst thing to get this far and have one of you—just *one* of you give in to a bad influence.

Philip: We'll just keep away from them.

Teacher: No.

Charles: If we're not allowed to go spread out, then they'll think we're still crazy.

John: I know.

Nicole: Regular kids don't do that.

John: I know. I'll feel like a baby.

Teacher: I just want our class to be together. I think it's safer. If anything happens at that zoo, they'll look at me first—"What did your kids do?" If you're with me, I can say quite clearly, "Nothing." I can say there is nothing that you did. I can vouch for anything that happens. You get the freedom, I get my protection. I do not feel protected letting you go. That makes me feel unprotected.

John: We're not nuts. We're not nuts.

Teacher: No, I know you're not nuts, however . . .

John: You think we're nuts. That's how you're treating us.

Teacher: No, I don't think you're nuts.

John: I'm going to feel like a baby.

Philip: Teacher, every time we want something we have to vote on it. Then how come we can't vote on . . .

Teacher: That's true. That's true. But at this point I'm going to have to use my teacher perogative and say this limit I've got to set. This, I'm not going to allow anyone to vote on. However, I'm going to leave you your freedom to move. You're not going to be all tied up. I just want you within eye distance . . . It's not that I'm saying I don't trust you. I do personally trust you. But I want this protection for me.

Philip: What could possibly go wrong?

John: That's what I say. We can't *die*.

Thomas: Like, if something happens to us and you're not around to see it, then that means that you can't do nothing about it.

Teacher: Right. If something goes wrong I am directly responsible. I want to be able to vouch for this class. I have stuck with you this far and I'm *not* going to let it go now. I can't do that. If you feel that you can't go under those conditions, we can vote not to go on the trip; but if we go on the trip, those are the conditions I've *got* to have.

Analysis. Once again, the students exhibited a strong Stage–3 sense of their readiness to be treated as normal early adolescents. They wanted to prove that they could be trusted to act age-appropriately in a nonsupervised, public environment. Only Thomas (last student comment) sympathized with the teacher's concern that someone might be influenced to his detriment by an outside source. All of the other students verbalized confidence in their ability to control themselves.

To review, the norm of Act Your Age was first proposed in the October 13 Class Meeting when the teacher exhorted the pupils to act their age during music class. The norm did not resurface until this meeting—and at a far more sophisticated level. The issue was no longer one of acting age-appropriately in a music class geared to accommodate special-needs children, but of acting age-appropriately in a public environment incognizant of any special needs they might have. The Act-Your-Age norm at this meeting was Stage 3, Phase 3: the students expected that they would adhere to prosocial behavioral standards at the zoo.

Outcome. The class voted unanimously to go to the zoo under the teacher's conditions. The zoo day, however, found the teacher having to relinquish her control and letting them go off on their own. The results of this action are reported in the following anecdotal records.

Anecdotal Records
On May 17 the class joined several others for its trip to the zoo. Although this teacher had made them agree to stay together for fear something would go wrong, it was clear when the group got to the zoo that they needed to be given free rein. Everyone, therefore, agreed upon a time to meet at the end of the school day and then scattered, mostly in pairs. When the day was over and the class had regrouped, the teacher found the students to be happy, relaxed, and well balanced. They reported having had a most enjoyable day. The teacher also discovered that Thomas had spurned Andrew's partnership (which she had been careful to arrange) and had gone off with a previous acquaintance. The next day was Thomas's last day in this teacher's room.

That day, as was his custom, Thomas arrived late to school. Instead of coming to the classroom, he went directly to the crisis teacher. The principal joined the crisis teacher and informed Thomas that she had an opening in another classroom. Did he care to fill it? (A child, Lloyd, from that classroom had been spending his days exclusively in the crisis classroom, and the principal had been looking for an opportunity to place him elsewhere. She now wanted to switch him and Thomas; her full motivation for this was revealed only later. See Anecdotal Records following May 18 Class Meeting.) Thomas declined her offer, so she sent him up to the room.

In the room the class was preparing to take its customary weekly vocabulary test—an activity in which Thomas had been participating. The test was taken, the English lesson was taught, and the class left for lunch. Thomas never entered the room. Evidently he had stood in the hallway for the forty-five minutes the academic work was taking place and had, at the end of that time, returned to the crisis classroom, reporting that he had been afraid to enter the class. He ate lunch in the crisis room, returning to this teacher's classroom only as the class was preparing to receive its end-of-the-week treat of fifty cents each and a trip to the store.

The teacher, who was totally unaware of the student-switching plot but who did know that Thomas had been in the building since 9:00 A.M. (the assistant had seen him sitting in the crisis classroom), questioned Thomas's motives for waiting through the morning work and appearing for the treat. Thomas became angry—even vile (something he hadn't done in almost two months) and spat out, "They're tired of you! They're tired of you! And you're going to get a big surprise!" He then said that he could leave, and the teacher opened the door for him to do so. Together they went to the crisis classroom. There, feeling protected and confident, Thomas openly admitted he had come to the room only for his fifty cents and that, since he had gone to the zoo, he didn't care what he did now.

The principal arrived, called the teacher aside, and accused her of telling Thomas he could not come into the classroom if he arrived late in the mornings. The principal stated that because of this, he had been afraid to come into the room. This was completely untrue. Thomas had been arriving one to two hours late every day for the past month, and this teacher had never commented upon his late entry.

May 18, Class Meeting

Issue. Thomas was discussed in the afternoon's class meeting:

Teacher: Thomas was told this morning, evidently, that he had an option to leave the classroom—and evidently there must have been some plan to move Lloyd up here whenever there was an opportunity to do so. The principal did tell me that Thomas was told this, so I think what happened was, Thomas came up to get out of us what he could get out of us.

Assistant: Um hum.

Teacher: And when his bluff was called, that was when he got *really* (hostile), which is unlike him (recently). If he hadn't known that he had the option of leaving, he never would have done it.

Assistant: No, and that's why he said he had a surprise for us.

Teacher: Yes, he knew then.

Assistant: Well, when I was on my way to lunch, she (the principal) stopped me and said that when Thomas came in this morning, he came right to her and said he was afraid to come into the classroom because I had told him if he came late again, he was not to come into the classroom. I said, "I did not say it like that. I told Thomas that when he was going to be late to get someone to let us know. The lunch count is supposed to be in at 9:00. When he comes in here at 10:30 and 11:00 I don't know whether to order him a lunch or not. You can't ask him what he wants for lunch without his getting vile and carrying on. And then, when you order just whatever, he gets mad," I said, "so I have learned to just leave Thomas alone."

Teacher: I think the whole thing is a charade. I feel that from the beginning (this morning) they knew that Thomas was sneaking out. Thomas wasn't upset. Thomas hadn't been upset. Thomas had a fantastic day at the zoo.

Peter: If he was upset, he would look it.

Teacher: Thomas had a fantastic day yesterday. Thomas has been getting along with people fine. No one's been down on him this past month and a half.

Someone: Um hum (throughout the speech above)

John: Nobody has been.

Philip: Maybe he used us just to go to the zoo.

Assistant: I told the principal he was using her, too. I said, "He's pulling your leg." I said, "He's a con person. He uses you to get what he wants. He did not want to do any work."

Teacher: . . . . She said, "He came up and he was afraid to come in the classroom." I said, "Wait, wait a minute. What time did you send Thomas up to the classroom?'' She said, ''10:15.'' I said, ''Afraid? We were having a vocabulary test at 10:15. He wasn't afraid to come in here [for the reasons the principal was intimating]. He didn't want to take his vocabulary test.''

David: I just thought of something. He was afraid to take the test.

Peter: Thought he would get a bad mark.

Teacher: He hadn't studied. He hadn't done what he was supposed to do . . . Which means he stood out there the whole time, until we were all finished the test, English, everything, and then went down there and said, ''Oh, I'm scared.''

Peter: And then when I went by he's sitting there like this (imitating Thomas's smugness).

Assistant: When I told her, she said, ''Oh, I have no doubt that Thomas is not always speaking the truth.''

Teacher: Always! I walked by at lunch and he was sitting there with his legs stretched out, comfortable and calm, drinking soda . . . whatever they give him. He likes his iced tea.

John: Iced tea, man! That would *never* happen to us!

Peter: Um hum.

Assistant: He sure was. That's why I decided I was going to *take* him a lunch ticket (instead of asking him to come with the class).

Teacher: And then he's up here for recess and his fifty cents.

Peter: He goes down there and takes candy from the jar. He opens up the filing cabinet and he takes the candy out.

Philip: You know, the crisis teacher likes him a lot. They have an understanding.

Assistant: I say that's his problem. Everybody caters to Thomas and he's using them.

Teacher: The thing is, he's never going to get any better. It wasn't until I finally came down on him like a bolt out of God that he finally got better. No one had ever done that with him before.

John: Uh uh.

Teacher: No one had told him he *had* to quit pushing people down stairs, cussing people out, and throwing scissors at them. They always said, "Ah, Thomas, let's understand him." That doesn't work.

John: I was helping him for awhile there, remember? I was sitting right next to him for a while.

Teacher: I know.

John: And I was helping him. And then he turned on me.

Peter: Yeah, he turned on me when he pushed me down the stairs.

Philip: When he gets what he wants from people, then he starts beating the heck out of them.

John: He turned on me! Remember that time that he was sitting there and I helped him with his problems?

Philip: It's like catching a fish, eating it, and throwing away the bones or something.

Teacher: Yes.

John: Yes.

Teacher: That's *exactly* how he treats people. People are not supposed to be treated like that. And I feel that they're wrong in their dealing with him.

Analysis. In this interchange the members of the class expressed their disapproval of Thomas's misuse of them. His lack of care for or true commitment to the community was viewed with disfavor. For these reasons the conversation reflected a Stage–3 sense of community valuing. In contrast to this were Thomas's actions and words, both of which reflected a Stage–2, manipulative attitude towards his class.

Anecdotal Records
Later that day the teacher expressed to the principal her dismay at the impression the principal or someone had left with Thomas concerning the administration's feelings towards her ("They're tired of you!"). She strongly felt that the principal should have brought the matter and Thomas to her so that all three of them could have discussed the situation openly

and honestly. The teacher felt compromised by lies she had not been allowed to refute.

At this, the principal admitted that she (the principal) did not want to keep Thomas the next year; that she wished the regular-school-district representative had taken him and put him ''anywhere''; that if Thomas acted up at all in his new (loosely structured) classroom she would get rid of him; and that she might try to squeeze him into the local special school for juvenile delinquents, even though he had not reached the required age. Since both the principal and the teacher were leaving the following year (the principal to retirement, the teacher to graduate school) there would be no one in the building who could handle Thomas. She felt it important, therefore, to get him out of the school this year so her successor wouldn't have to deal with him.

The exchange of pupils took place and Lloyd entered this teacher's classroom. The class was initially dismayed at the prospect of receiving Lloyd, because he was several years younger than they and because he was such an inept athlete. However, the comparable mildness of his behavior soon counterbalanced the handicap they feared he would be on the playing field. John spent several days playing stick-ball with Lloyd and, after many trials, Lloyd's catching skills improved. It was clear, however, that Lloyd was not geared to the do-or-die baseball games the class was accustomed to playing, and he made no effort to join them. Lloyd seemed content to be left alone. All in all, it was a fortunate change of students.

The school year was coming to an end. Peter made a wonderful and warm year book which everyone illustrated and in which everyone described himself. Philip had found a close friend in Charles and they spent every free minute together. John remained a positive group member who spent much of his time taking care of the other class members.

Thomas finished the year in his new classroom—never interacting with his old classmates again. He quickly figured out that he had been manipulated by the principal and cursed her roundly two days later. Moreover, he foiled her scheme to get him out of the building. He controlled himself, completed the year, and returned to Valley Brook the following year (see Follow-Up, Appendix B).

Andrew's maturity was attracting attention. He was called upon by the crisis-classroom teacher to calm down the younger acting-out children in the school who idolized him; the principal of the other school called upon Andrew to help him with an emergency building repair. Unfortunately, however, Andrew's ego outstripped his maturity; and his bragging was angering his peers.

Nicole was confronting some deep, long-term resentments toward family members and reqired a great deal of talking to. This teacher spent two hours one morning reminding Nicole that she had a hopeful future: she was returning to regular-class placement for the first time in years; within five years she would be a free adult; she *had* to gather the strength to follow her chosen path to its end. The next day Nicole came into the classroom with her hair beautifully permed.

Field Day was a Valley Brook tradition. The entire school gathered outside on the playing fields for a day of sports competition. It was a wonderful day—the best Field Day this teacher had ever had in six years of Field Days: this class of seven contestants walked away with twelve ribbons. Unfortunately, Charles and Andrew tied for the most blue ribbons and had a play-off game one week later. The play-off was judged by the principal and the gym teacher, both of whom had expressed strong disapproval of Andrew's attitude. They declared Charles the winner. The class cheered Charles wildly. Andrew's bragging had so alienated them that they seized this opportunity to pay him back. Andrew was broken hearted but, after calming down, he listened with understanding as this teacher identified the cause of the group's censure of him: his inflated ego.

The second Valley Brook end-of-the-year tradition was a day of swimming and picnicking at a country lodge with a swimming pool, basketball courts, and acres of hills and woods. The previous year several older children had gotten lost in the woods. This year this teacher required the class to agree not to go into the woods without an adult. Philip refused to agree, so the class sat in the classroom—picnic and swimming paraphernalia all around, the rest of the school boarding the buses—in a stalemate. Philip wouldn't agree, and the teacher wouldn't go anywhere unless he agreed. Soon the buses were going to have to leave. Thank goodness for David who kept saying, "That's not so bad. You have to stay with the teacher in regular school." *Finally* Philip gave in, and the class ran to the waiting buses.

Again, this picnic day turned out to be the best picnic day this teacher had experienced in six years. No one wandered off; no one argued or fought; Philip and Charles did all the cooking. Lloyd's mother had baked a huge "graduation" cake, which the class cut in unison while wishing each other luck in their individual futures. It was a picture-perfect afternoon.

All that remained was the ending. The students gradually dropped away. Each day of the final week found fewer and fewer returning; the last half day only Andrew, Peter, and Lloyd arrived. Lloyd mopped the classroom floor, and Andrew announced he had come to help the teacher finish moving the heavy boxes of school material to her car: "Leave all the heavy work to me, Teacher." Peter presented the teacher with a beautiful oriental poetry book of his which she had admired all year. At

11:00 A.M. their buses arrived, they said good-bye, they rode away. The students had been launched. Would that they might fly!

Notes

1. Adapted from C. Power, "The Moral Atmosphere of the School: A Method for Analyzing Community Meetings" (Qualifying Paper, Harvard Graduate School of Education, 1978).

2. For a full exposition of the stages of collective normative values and sense of community valuing, the reader is referred to Ann Higgins, Clark Power, and Lawrence Kohlberg, "Student Judgments of Responsibility and the Moral Atmosphere of High Schools: A Comparative Study," in *Morality, Moral Development, and Moral Behavior: Basic Issues in Theory and Research,* ed. William Kurtiness (New York: John Wiley & Sons, in press).

4 Conclusions

Here the author summarizes her thoughts on factors that contribute to a healthy classroom environment, stimulate what is most noble in students, and oppose that which is detrimental to their optimal development.

Quality leadership is the sine qua non; because of its congruence with the law of evolution, Plato's concept of philosopher-kings is a sound one. Only the finest should teach, and they should exercise strong initiative.

Second, a teacher should never hold a class back for a student who clearly functions below them. The law of evolution states that all things are to progress toward their highest manifestation on any level, and an objective observer can easily detect a hierarchy on any plane: experience has more to offer than inexperience; adulthood is more advanced than childhood. When the higher element rules the lower, the lower comes under its guidance and changes for the better. When the higher is held in check by the tyranny of the low, evolution is thwarted; chaos reigns.

Next, any serious educational effort must stand on a system of unequivocal values. To speak of an educational program without values is a contradiction in terms, since values, even when not explicitly stated, are implicit in every action—in every choice. High or low, in a classroom they draw like energy from the children they touch. High ends are not attained without conscious, directed effort. The law of entropy informs this truth: matter, without a directional application of energy, deteriorates into an inert uniformity. As with all truth, this law operates within the spiritual, mental, astral, and physical planes—including the schoolroom.

Under the aegis of a carefully selected set of values, definite activities which stimulate positive growth can be instituted. In this teacher's experience, two powerful activities of this nature are group sports and class meetings. Intelligently monitored, they can actively promote integrity, responsibility, compromise, cooperation, evaluative ability, role-taking skill, the ability to take the long view, and willingness to work for the welfare of the group. It is this teacher's firm belief that without these two activities the experimental class would have remained a conglomeration of individuals who could never have integrated into a normal school setting.

Fourth, academic achievement must be stressed in classrooms for the emotionally disturbed. A primary purpose of education is the transmission of knowledge. One of the biggest handicaps emotionally disturbed children can have is an inability to compete academically. It is not enough to restore these children to emotional stability. The teacher must also equip them with the skills necessary to function successfully in a normal academic setting, for academic competence in such a setting contributes greatly to emotional stability.

The ultimate function of education is to make man all that he is capable of being. To attain this end, an educational program must, then, provide the finest leadership, give priority to the noblest and best in its students, profess and pursue the highest of values (love of reason, of truth, of goodness, of serving universal well-being), and foster perceptual clarity and intellectual acumen in those it seeks to serve.

Appendixes

Appendix A
Developmental
Measures, Results, and
Discussion

An amoral group of students had entered this teacher's classroom in September. Throughout the fall months they seemed utterly incapable of forming a mutually supportive group operating in positive strength. By June, however, they had achieved this goal. The transition had been neither quick nor easy. Belief that an ideal could be actualized, perseverance through enormous obstacles, and sheer necessity (income for the teacher; state law for the students) were the principal factors in bringing the year to its successful conclusion.

This section reports the measures used to assess (1) moral reasoning, (2) social role-taking, and (3) academic performance, together with the data analysis procedures. The growth of the class is then documented by (1) pre- and posttest results in the moral, social, and academic realms, (2) the development of group norms, and (3) the development and merger of two subgroups.

Measures Used

All students in the experimental class were tested in the following areas using the following measures:

Moral Reasoning

Kohlberg's Standard Moral Judgment Interview, Forms A and B, were administered orally to all students in the experimental class. Approximately half of the students received Form A on the pretest (September, 1978) and Form B on the posttest (May, 1979), and vice versa.[1] (A copy of both forms can be found in Appendix F.) It is important to note here that age-appropriate reasoning for early adolescents is Stage 2/3.

Social Role-Taking

Chandler's Perspective-Taking Task,[2] which measures nonegocentric thinking, was administered to all students in the experimental class as a pretest in September, 1978, and as a posttest in May, 1979. This task involves interpretation of a series of pictures that portray an emotion-laden interpersonal situation.

One story sequence is of a boy (a) building a sand castle at the beach, (b) being very proud of it, (c) having a girl ride her bicycle through it, (d) becoming quite angry, (e) stomping home, (f) meeting his younger brother who happily shows him a house of cards he has been building, and (g) blowing the younger brother's house of cards down.

The second is of a young girl (a) kissing a man good-bye at an airport, (b) sadly waving to a plane aloft, (c) climbing a fence at the airport—still waving, (d) walking despondently home, (e) happily receiving a package from a mailman, (f) opening the package in front of the mailman, (g) finding in it a toy airplane, and (h) crying while the mailman looks on.

Each student was asked, by this researcher, first to pretend he was the older boy (or the young girl) and to tell the story from that point of view, and then to pretend he was the younger boy (or the mailman) and to tell the story from that point of view.

Academic Pretests

Reading and Mathematics Grade levels in reading and mathematics for all but one student had been measured and recorded by the previous year's teachers. These levels had been determined by two assessments:

1. The McCracken Oral Reading Inventory, which provides grade-level equivalents.
2. A diagnostic mathematics test (designed and copyrighted by the host school), which identifies a student's strengths and weaknesses in particular skill areas; grade-level placement is determined by the teacher.

(Peter, who had not attended this school before, was pretested on these two measures in September, 1978.)

Spelling Spelling grade levels were determined by a graded spelling test compiled by Towson State College.[3] This test was administered to all students in the experimental class in September, 1978.

Academic Posttests

Reading and Mathematics

1. The Metropolitan Standardized Achievement Test—Form H

2. The McCracken Oral Reading Inventory

Spelling The Towson State College graded spelling test.

Two-Year Follow-Up Data

The two-year follow-up data were obtained through Kohlberg's Moral Judgment Interviews (Forms A and B, administered orally), Chandler's Social Role-Taking Task (1980 only), report-card grades, and personal interviews.

Data Analysis Procedures

The *t*-test has been run on the Moral Judgment pre- and posttest mean change scores to determine statistical significance.

Moral Reasoning

Pre- to posttest change in moral reasoning has been determined by blind scoring of all interviews by trained scorers at the Center for Moral Education, Harvard Graduate School of Education.

Global stage, "moral maturity," and "moral-maturity scale" scores for each subject are presented. In most cases two or three global stages have been assigned per subject per interview time. This indicates that at least 25 percent of the subject's responses fell at that stage or at those stages. A third stage (presented in parentheses) has been assigned if it represents 10 percent or more of the subject's responses. The stage scores have been weighted and averaged to yield a moral-maturity score (MMS), designed, in part, for easy presentation of ordinal data. The MMS ranges from 100 (Stage 1) to 500 (Stage 5).[4]

Social Role-Taking

Pre- to posttest change in perspective-taking as measured by the Chandler Picture Stories has been analyzed. The student is evaluated on his ability to

1. Attribute accurate motives to the actions of another from data presented in cartoon form.

2. Draw reasonable conclusions about the probable thought processes of another who must reason from incomplete data (from data presented in cartoon form).

Pretest and Posttest Results

Moral Reasoning

Table A–1 presents individual pretest and posttest Global Stage scores. As can be seen, all but one student progressed in moral-reasoning stage. On the pretest, five of the seven students used a high percentage of Stage–1 and Stage–2 reasoning (at least 25 percent of their responses falling at these two stages); only two students exhibited a high percentage of Stage 3. On the posttest, five of the seven students used a high percentage of Stage–2 and Stage–3 reasoning. No one used a high percentage of Stage 1.

Table A–2 presents individual and mean pretest–to–posttest change in Moral Maturity Score (MMS). The mean change in MMS was 56

Table A–1
Global Stage Change Scores 1978–1979

Students	1978 Pretest	1979 Posttest
John	1	2/3
Matthew	2/1 (3)	3/2
Andrew	2/1	2 (1)
Thomas	3/2	2 (1)
Philip	2/1	3/2 (4)
Peter	2/1	3/2
Nicole	2/3	2/3

Table A–2
Moral-Maturity Change Scores 1978–1979

Students	1978 Pretest	1979 Posttest	Change
John	120	242	+122
Matthew	175	258	+83
Andrew	160	185	+25
Thomas	254	197	−57
Philip	163	270	+107
Peter	160	264	+104
Nicole	220	231	+11
Mean	179	235	+56

points. A *t*-test for paired observations indicates that this change score is significant at the .05 level of significance.

Social Role-Taking

The social role-taking tasks (Chandler Picture Stories) were passed with ease by Nicole, Matthew, Philip, and Peter during pretesting and post-testing (Table A–3.) John passed the pretest (The Boy and his Sandcastle) without difficulty, but on the posttest (The Girl and the Airplane) he initially focused on sex-role stereotyping rather than the relational affect (''She starts crying cause she gets an airplane. Girls play with dolls, not airplanes.'') Andrew passed the pretest and posttest but required more probing than did most of the other students before he made the affective connections. Thomas experienced the greatest difficulty with this task. On the pretest (The Boy and his Sandcastle) he could not spontaneously give a third-party account. In fact, he confused the actions of the older and younger brothers in interpreting the picture sequence and had to be guided in separating them.

Because Thomas's pretest responses were so unusual, his pretest interview is presented here in full:

Thomas: The boy was building a sandcastle. And he got it done. Then the girl on the bike came and ran it over. Then the boy was mad, so he went home. He seen his brother build a house out of cards; he blew it down. The boy started crying. Then he left.

Teacher: Now, pretend you are the younger boy in the story. Tell me the story from his point of view.

Table A–3
Role-Taking Task, 1978–1979

Students	1978 Pretest	1979 Posttest
John	Pass	Marginal pass
Matthew	Pass	Pass
Andrew	Marginal pass	Marginal pass
Thomas	Fail	Marginal pass
Philip	Pass	Pass
Peter	Pass	Pass
Nicole	Pass	Pass

Thomas: What? Tell it over?

Teacher: What do you think? If you are going to tell the story from the little boy's point of view, how would you do that?

Thomas: I don't know.

Teacher: Where do you think you would start to tell the story if you were the little boy?

Thomas: Right here. (Pointed to the appropriate picture frame.)

Teacher: OK.

Thomas: He walked in the house. He built the house made of cards. Blew it down. Just left.

Teacher: OK. Now, that was still mostly about the big boy. Pretend you are this child.

Thomas: What would I be?

Teacher: Tell me the story from his point of view.

Thomas: Built a house of cards. Left it sitting there. (Long pause)

Teacher: And what's he thinking? What's the little boy thinking in this picture?

Thomas: How fine he built it.

Teacher: Yes. So, now what is he thinking?

Thomas: He's mad.

Teacher: What's he thinking over here?

Thomas: Angry.

Teacher: All right, Thomas. Do you think the little brother *knew* why the big brother kicked down his house of cards?

Thomas: No.

Teacher: Why not?

Thomas: He wasn't there.

Teacher: Do you think the big brother knew the little brother didn't know what had happened?

Thomas: No.

Teacher: What do you think the big brother thought?

Thomas: He thought it was him.

Teacher: Who did what?

Thomas: Knocked his sandcastle over. Unless he took it out on him.

Teacher: Yes, maybe he did.

In his posttest Thomas separated the characters correctly but ignored the affect. After one probe, however, he passed the task.

Academics

Table A–4 presents the pretest and posttest results in the academic realm. The numbers represent grade-level equivalents. For example 4.5 is equivalent to fourth grade, fifth month.

Discussion

The greatest pretest–to–posttest advances in the moral realm were made by John, from Stage 1 to Stage 2/3; Matthew, from Stage 2/1(3) to Stage 3/2; Philip, from Stage 2/1 to Stage 3/2(4); and Peter, from Stage 2/1 to 3/2. Andrew gained in moral reasoning from Stage 2/1 to 2(1) but failed to reach an age-appropriate level of 2/3. His communication difficulties and slower social understanding (evidenced in his performance on the role-taking task) are believed by this researcher to be the reasons for the absence of Stage–3 reasoning in his moral-judgment posttest. Nicole entered in September reasoning at an age-appropriate level and stayed at that level.

Table A–4
Academic Achievement Grade Levels, Pre- to Posttest Change

	Reading			Mathematics			Spelling		
	Sept. '78	Apr. '79	Change	Sept. '78	Apr. '79	Change	Sept. '78	Apr. '79	Change
John	6.0[a]	7.0[a] 6.8[b]	0.9	4.0	6.6[b]	2.6	5.0	7.0	2.0
Matthew[c]									
Andrew	4.0[a]	5.0[a] 5.9[b]	1.0	4.5	6.9[b]	2.4	5.0	7.0	2.0
Thomas	3.5[a]	4.0[a] 4.5[b]	0.8	3.0	3.2[b]	0.2	4.0	4.0	0.0
Philip	5.0[a]	6.0[a] 6.0[b]	1.0	5.0	7.4[b]	2.4	Unrecorded	5.0	—
Peter	6.0[a]	7.0[a] 7.0[b]	1.0	4.0	4.6[b]	0.6	5.0	7.5	2.5
Nicole	4.5[a]	6.0[a] 6.2[b]	1.6	5.0	6.4[b]	1.4	4.0	6.0	2.0
Mean gain	4.8	5.9	1.1	4.3	5.8	1.5	4.6	6.3	1.7

[a]McCracken Oral Reading Inventory.
[b]Metropolitan Standardized Achievement Test, Form H.
[c]Not available. Left February 28 before posttesting.

Thomas was the sole student to regress in his moral-reasoning stage. A possible explanation for this regression follows.

Thomas's pretest performance on the social role-taking task, when compared to his reasoning on the cognitively based moral task, highlights a disastrous split between his social understanding and his abstract moral-reasoning ability. Thomas pretested at moral stage 3/2, indicating a sophisticated cognitive competency. On the role-taking pretest, however, he could not separate the reality of the older boy from that of the younger; he even attributed the destruction of the older boy's sandcastle to the younger boy when the picture sequence clearly indicated that that was not the case. Thomas's warped view of the role-taking task was reflective of his warped view of real-life interpersonal situations.

This teacher equates Thomas's regression on the moral-judgment interview in May with his ability to control himself sufficiently to prevent expulsion at the end of the school year. Thomas's Stage 3/2 reasoning in September represented, in a sense, a false reality—one divorced from the realm of interpersonal understanding and behavior. It is felt that the Stage—2(1) reasoning evidenced in May represented the merger of these two realms, a restructuring of Thomas's entire system, and a building of a new foundation from which both parts of himself could grow as a whole.

The group's academic gain was quite good—easily comparable to or surpassing the gain a normal student is expected to make in a school year.

The Development of Group Norms

This researcher has identified seven major norms. These norms and the months in which they were active are presented in Table A–5. As can be seen, the two norms which were most active were The Group is One and No Name Calling. The norms Separate the Deviant Member(s) from

Table A–5
Group Norms

Norm	Sept.	Oct.	Nov.	Dec.	Jan.	Mar.	Apr.	May
1. The Group is One			X	X	X	X	X	
2. No Name Calling			X	X		X	X	
3. Separate Deviant Member(s) from Group		X						
4. Act Your Age		X						X
5. Mind Your Own Business	X	X						
6. No Snapping Out				X		X		
7. Eat with Manners		X						

the Group, Mind Your Own Business, and Eat with Manners ceased to operate after the month of October, while those of Act Your Age and No Snapping Out resurfaced at varying intervals.

Table A–6 follows the progression of these norms in phase and stage, as well as the stage of community valuing.

The seven norms have been classified under two headings: (1) norms of separation and (2) norms of integration.

Norms of Separation

Mind Your Own Business and Separate the Deviant Member(s) from the Group fall into the category of norms of separation. Both had been dropped from the norm repertoire by November. The first, Mind Your Own Business, disappeared when Keith left the class. In actuality, such a norm was impossible to enact, given the smallness of the group (between seven and nine students), the intensity and the length of group-member contact (six hours a day, five days a week), and the interactive activities instituted by the teacher to stimulate development (Sharing Time, class meetings, dilemma discussions).

Because the group was so small, the Separate-the Deviant-Member(s)-from-the-Group norm was also impractical. The separation of some segment of the class for any length of time too greatly affected the whole. For example, a certain number of people was instrumentally necessary to play a satisfying game of catch, or tag, or baseball; and the gym games depended upon the cooperative interaction of *all* group members. Too, the teacher's refusal to split the group for any reason (October 13 Class Meeting) and the teacher's and the assistant's continual call for group unity worked against the acceptance of this norm of separation.

Norms of Integration

The integrative norms were Eat with Manners, The Group is One, No Name Calling, No Snapping Out, and Act Your Age. The majority of these norms were proposed by the teacher during the fall months, and mostly at Stage 3. It was not until spring that they were completely accepted by the students.

Eat with Manners As observed in Chapter 3, the norm Eat with Manners was already operating at Phase 3 in early October, suggesting that it had existed within individual students' repertoires before their entry into the

Table A–6
Progression of Norms and Community Valuing

Date	Issue	Norm	Phase	Stage	Stage of Com. Val.	Notes
9/18/78	Rules discussion	Mind Your Own Business	1			Keith
10/6/78	Lunch-table eating	1. Eat with Manners	5, 6b	3		Nicole, Peter, John
		2. Separate the Deviant Member(s) from the Group	2			Everyone but Keith
		3. Mind Your Own Business				
10/13/78	A. Splitting the class during music because of bad behavior	1. Act Your Age	1	2		Keith
		2. Take Other Class Members into Account	1	3		Teacher
		3. Separate the Deviant Member(s) from the Group	1	Guess 2		Teacher
	B. Philip's speaking nastily to the teacher; The teacher's asking the class for help				0	John, Peter, Thomas
						"It's not our class"
						The Students
11/3/78	A. Class ball	The Group is One (on the Playing Field)	1	2	2	Teacher
				3	"Subgroups take turns"	Assistant
11/15/78	Name calling	1. Ignore Name Calling	4	(Criticism of) 2		Peter (proposal)
						Class (by vote)
		2. No Name Calling	1			Whole class
12/1/78	A. Name calling	No Name Calling	3		3	Teacher (3 people, take points)
					2	Whole class (3 people, take points)
	B. Nicole, Peter, John, and Matthew on playing field arguing: Subgroup development				3/2	Peter, John
					2	Nicole
	C. How to greet the new student, Wayne				3/2	John, Philip, Peter

Table A–6 *(continued)*

Date	Issue	Norm	Phase	Stage	Stage of Com. Val.	Notes
12/18/78	Special meeting: Do you care about the class?				2/3	Everyone but Matthew, Teacher
		1. The Group Is One (in Internal Strength)	1	3		
		2. No Snapping Out	1			
1/26/79	A. Philip Attacking subgroup for receiving special privileges	The Group Is One (in Close Friendship)	1	3		Peter, Teacher
	B. Discussion about Matthew's severely disturbed behavior	1. Care	3	3	3	Peter, Andrew, Nicole, John
		2. The Group Is One (in Care for a Troubled Class Member)	2	3	3	Andrew, Nicole
3/16/79	Race: Philip's bringing Thomas to subgroup baseball game	No Snapping Out	3	3	3 (Subgroup)	Nicole, John, Peter
3/23/79	Outside adult reaction to group's improvement		3	3	3	Whole class
3/30/79	A. Name calling	No Name Calling	6b, 3			Whole class
	B. Playing as a whole class during recess	The Group Is One (on the Playing Field)	1	3		Teacher, John, assistant
4/3/79	The class has been separated in the lunchroom			3	3	Whole class
		No Name Calling	5			David, Peter
		The Group Is One (in Responsibility)	3	3	3	David, Peter, John Nicole
4/20/79	Vote to remain at the back lunch table	The Group is One (in Internal Strength)	3	3	3	Whole class
4/27/79	Playing as a whole class during recess	The Group Is One (on the Playing Field)	2	3	2	Whole class
5/11/79	Zoo trip	Act Your Age	3	3	3	Whole Class
5/18/79	Thomas's exit from the classroom		3	3	3	Whole class (but Thomas)

experimental classroom. Matthew's transgressions were immediately and strongly censured; the issue did not arise again.

The Group is One The norm The Group is One was the central norm of the year and was active in the discussion of several different issues (see Table A–7).

The first version of the norm—The Group is One on the Playing Field—played, perhaps, the most important role in the group's integration. During the fall months it was practically impossible to implement; the students were too disturbed and interacted at too low a stage. Self-coordination of teams and the voluntary cooperation of team members requires the Stage–3 ability to adjust one's actions to fit the accurately perceived positions of others. The students were unable to do this in the fall; they required strong adult leadership (such as the gym teacher provided) within a highly structured playing situation to be able to play as a group.

By the end of March, crippling disturbances and preconventional interactions were no longer the barriers to group integration on the playing field. Now the barrier was the power hold of Nicole over her subgroup. Nicole's determination to maintain her uncontested leadership was unopposed by anyone but the teacher and the assistant in the March 30

Table A–7
Versions of the Norm, The Group Is One

1. The Group Is One on the Playing Field.

Date	Phase	Stage
11/3/78	1	2/3
3/30/79	1	3
4/27/79	2	3

2. The Group Is One in Internal Strength.

Date	Phase	Stage
12/18/78	1	3
4/20/79	3	3

3. The Group Is One in Close Friendship.

Date	Phase	Stage
1/26/79	1	3

4. The Group Is One in Care for a Troubled Class Member.

Date	Phase	Stage
1/26/79	2	3

5. The Group Is One in Sharing Responsibility.

Date	Phase	Stage
4/3/79	3	3

Class Meeting. The norm The Group is One on the Playing Field remained in the proposal phase until after the powerfully unifying isolation of the class in the lunchroom.

When group unity on the playing field was finally accepted in the April 27 Class Meeting, it was done with ease. A limit on Nicole's power was quickly and effectively instituted and the class fully integrated, with Stage–3 skill, without further incident.

The acceptance of the second version, The Group is One on Internal Strength, is an interesting example of the truth that thought precedes action. In the December 18 Special Class Meeting the class first discussed the meaning of strength, that is, that of unity in following a "high road." In the April 20 Class Meeting the students voted to remain separated from the rest of the school in the lunchroom in order to maintain and to foster its prosocial community which *had* followed the "high road." The December "mental picture" had become the April reality.

A third version of the norm The Group is One in Close Friendship never moved beyond the proposal phase in class meetings. Observed student interactions during the spring months, however, convince this teacher that the norm was eventually accepted. The fourth and fifth versions were the only two to manifest immediately at a phase higher than Phase 1: the former, The Group is One in Care for a Troubled Class Member, was at Phase 2 in January; and the latter, The Group is One in Sharing Responsibility, was at Phase 3 in April. This teacher was surprised at the students' comments during both of these meeting. She did not expect to hear such an outpouring of care for Matthew in January nor the self-criticism, acceptance of punishment, and concern for the prosocial image of Valley Brook in April. Both of these meetings were clear indications that the group had moved farther in solidifying a Stage–3 community than the teacher had realized.

There was no single meeting in which all aspects of The Group is One were explicitly accepted. It is felt by this teacher, however, that the official decision in the April 27 Class Meeting to unite on the playing field epitomized its attainment, simply because the group's unity and independence on the playing field was the longest in coming and the hardest to actualize.

No Name Calling There were three versions of the No Name Calling norm. The first—Ignore Name Calling—reigned for most of the fall. In the November 15 Class Meeting the students expressed their exasperation with name calling and asked the teacher for help in eliminating it. Also during that time (from the end of October into November) the teacher had launched a campaign against the students' speaking nastily to each other, and they had been making a conscious effort to stop.

Name calling persisted, however, and the implicit norm to ignore it (active since the beginning of the year) was not working. Because they feared misuse by their fellow classmates, the students did not accept the teacher's proposal in the November 15 Class Meeting to take points from the name caller if three people heard him. Instead, they reluctantly voted to make the implicit Stage–2 norm (Ignore Name Calling) an official policy, hoping that that would be a sufficient deterrent. It was not; and by the December 1 Class Meeting the students were ready to accept the teacher's November 15 proposal. Their immediate implementation of the new, more-stringent policy introduced the second version of the Name Calling norm, that is; No Name Calling.

This second version operated well until David entered the classroom in February. Then name calling again became an issue. It was not raised in a class meeting, however, until March 30 when Philip, quite unexpectedly, proposed a double-bind policy which the class voted unanimously to accept: Points would be taken from the name caller for calling the name and from the person who had been called the name if he did not ignore it. Thus, the Ignore-Name-Calling norm and the No-Name-Calling norm had been combined to create the third version.

It is felt by this teacher that the combination of the two versions of the Name-Calling norm was a strong statement by the class that it intended to uphold a Stag–3 community in which members treated each other well. Interestingly, this stringent policy preceded by two school days the cathartic separation of the class in the lunchroom for engaging in a name-calling battle with a student in another class. Perhaps the No-Name-Calling/Ignore-Name-Calling policy accepted on March 30 was an attempt by the students to stem a tide they intuitively knew was soon to engulf them.

No Snapping Out The norm of No Snapping Out was first indirectly proposed in the December 18 Special Class Meeting. At that meeting several students labeled violent strength as both sad and a weakness; the teacher equated it with following a low road. This was the first time the students had sufficiently separated themselves from the daily reality of explosive and intimidating violence to categorize it in such a clear and insightful way. The teacher introduced the element of choice: the class could choose to follow a high road and work as a group in sane strength (which included eliminating "snapping out") or to follow the low by embracing the explosive insanity which had been characteristic of the classroom until then. The conversation was not in the fairness form; therefore, no vote was taken. An impression had been made upon the students, however, because three of them entered the class the next morning announcing their intention to improve.

Between the proposal of the No-Snapping-Out norm and its explicit application, the teacher had a serious encounter with Thomas after he threatened to snap out on David and her. It became clear to the teacher (and probably to the students) that the administration would not or could not protect anyone in the class from Thomas's uncontrollable violence. In response the class began to devise ways to protect itself: the teacher threatened to show the head of Thomas's home a disparaging report she had written about his violent misuse of class members; she also visibly withdrew from personal contact with him. On March 16 the subgroup of Nicole, John, Peter, and David repelled Philip's attempt to integrate Thomas into their baseball game. They emphasized their fear of his snapping out on one of them as their reason for rejecting his team membership. In its actions and justifications the subgroup enacted the No-Snapping-Out norm at Phase 3, Stage 3. They expected it to be upheld, and they fought to ensure the well-being of all members of their playing team. In their actions they were also protecting Thomas, whether consciously or not, from himself.

Act Your Age The norm Act Your Age first appeared in the proposal phase in the October 13 Class Meeting. At that time the teacher exhorted the students to act their age in music class by cooperating with the music teacher whether they liked it or not. The norm did not appear again until the May 11 Class Meeting in the discussion of the upcoming zoo trip. Then, the students forcefully demonstrated their full understanding and acceptance of the norm and exhorted the teacher to treat them accordingly.

The May 11 interchange indicated the norm Act Your Age was operating at Phase 3, Stage 3: the students expected prosocial behavior from themselves. It also signaled the group's readiness to disperse and the individual students' readiness to reassemble with a different group of peers in the regular-school system.

In conclusion, the two norms of separation were dropped from the norm repertoire by November as inappropriate. Four of the five norms of integration remained in operation throughout most of the school year. The fifth integrative norm (Eat with Manners) had already been established by October and did not require further attention. The four integrative norms which continued all reached Stage 3, Phase 2 or 3, indicating that a Stage-3 community had been attained in the experimental classroom.

The Development and Merger of Two Subgroups

The subgroup of Nicole, Peter, and John was the first Stage-3 group to form within the experimental class. A second formed when the basketball twosome of Andrew and Philip was joined by Charles at the end of March. Within a month after the second group's formation the two groups united into a single Stage–3 community. This section traces the development of that community from the perspective of subgroups.

John, Peter, and Matthew formed the first subgroup in early October when they came together to play frisbee during lunch recess. It is hypothesized that these three came together for Stage–2 reasons: temporary concrete exchange and, occasionally, for protection from Thomas's aggression.

The first indication that Nicole, Peter, and John were compatible was their use of higher stage reasoning in the October 6 Class Meeting: these three were the only students to offer Stage–3 objections to Matthew's eating habits ("It's embarrassing to the class.") By early November Nicole had joined John, Peter, and Matthew for daily games of tag and kickball. The group's stage of interaction was not clear until the December 1 Class Meeting, however. At that time Peter and John exhorted Nicole to stop pushing them in the mud when she was angry and to treat them nicely and with respect (Stage–3 requests). Nicole, in response, justified her physical expression of anger in Stage–2 fairness terms: Peter and John were not recognizing her need to play with the ball on the playing field.

During the month of December when violence, resistance to school work, and highly disturbed behavior were very much in evidence, John, Peter, and Nicole became the "good kids." They moved their desks together to do their morning folder work. In the December 18 Class Meeting they were the first to answer "Yes" to the teacher's question, "Do you care about the classroom?," and Peter compared the class to a family. Matthew had dropped from the subgroup by December. Perhaps the severity of his disturbance prevented him from enjoying the sustained, positive human contact that the subgroup was beginning to offer its members.

By the end of January the subgroup was operating fully at Stage 3. Its members did everything together, including build an exclusive study area in the back of the room. The furor which this area engendered was a reaction to the negative aspects of Stage 3: cattiness and in-grouping and out-grouping. These negative aspects were vigorously opposed by the teacher, and they did not arise in that magnitude again.

It is felt that David's acceptance into the subgroup in February was due to his sunny, accommodating manner.

On March 16 the subgroup again demonstrated its Stage–3 nature by summarily rejecting Thomas's entry into a baseball game because they feared his violence. Physical expression of anger was now totally unacceptable. They were unwilling to compromise on the issue (terminating their game) until it was discussed in that afternoon's class meeting and an official policy which provided reasonable protection was established. This official policy (anyone could enter a game if he could control his violence; the first time someone did become violent, he would be barred from playing for one week) set the stage for the eventual integration of all class members into a single unit.

By March 30 Philip, Andrew, and the newly transferred student, Charles, had formed a playing group on the basketball court. (Philip had been playing with Andrew for many weeks, but it is hypothesized that Andrew's communication difficulties and reticent nature had prevented them from becoming close friends.) Charles's entry provided the alchemical fire which produced a second Stage–3 subgroup of Philip, Charles, and peripherally Andrew. Its solidification was almost instantaneous, showing Philip's and Charles's readiness to change. Philip had not been able to join the subgroup of Nicole, Peter, John, and David because his strong nature would have threatened Nicole's leadership; Charles had become a developmental "misfit" in his former class, far surpassing his classmates in social skill. Both of these boys were visibly overjoyed to come together.

In the March 30 Class Meeting the teacher, assistant, and John moved that the two subgroups merge on the playing field; but Nicole vehemently opposed it. Upon witnessing Nicole pounding on the table and screaming for the defeat of the motion, Philip rejected it too.

Two school days later the class was isolated in the lunchroom. The students and teachers drew closer together than they had ever been. The two subgroups united on the playing field. A clear note of unity was sounded in the April 27 Class Meeting when the students decided to secure community playing equipment so that no single person could rule the games. With that, the subgroups were no more and the group had become one as a Stage–3 community.

Notes

1. In Ann Colby, Lawrence Kohlberg, John Gibbs, and Marcus Lieberman, et. al., *The Measurement of Moral Judgment* (New York: Cambridge University Press, in press).

2. Michael Chandler and S. Greenspan, "Erzatz-Egocentrism: A Reply to H. Borke," *Developmental Psychology* 7 (1972): 104–106.

3. Joseph P. Gutkoska, *Diagnosis and Prescription: A Teacher's Guide for Developmental Reading* (Edison, New Jersey: Crown Publishers, Inc.), pp. 43–46.

4. Colby, et al., *Measurement*.

Appendix B
Follow-Up

During the two years following the intervention program, this researcher twice interviewed the original seven students (spring of 1980 and of 1981) and communicated with most of them several other times. What follows is a report of each student's progress in the personal, academic, and moral spheres. (The social role-taking task was dropped from the interview format in 1981 because all but John had shown full mastery of it in 1980.)

John

John was attending eighth grade in a regular junior high school. In January, 1980, this teacher spoke to a guidance counselor about John's academic progress and to the principal's secretary (who saw all the behavior-problem students in the school) about John's behavior. John had done well in both areas. He had received mostly B's and some C's on his first-semester report card. For the semester coming up he had received one deficiency report in math. Not once had John been referred to the principal's office for problem behavior.

In March, 1980, this teacher visited John at his home. He was still very small for his age—just under five feet tall—and complained that the larger boys at school were picking on him. John said that he was not as happy in this school; he spoke wistfully of his previous year's experience and suggested that the whole class meet for a picnic.

Although John's new school situation was socially trying, he was doing well academically. He had been placed in a reading resource room (which he didn't think he needed), but had received A's, B's, and C's on his last-semester's report card.

John's enjoyment came from his out-of-school church activities. He had sold the most tickets to a church function (thereby winning one-week's free tuition to the church's summer camp) and was now busily working to earn enough money to pay for a second week. John spoke several times with relief of being able to spend part of his summer in the country.

This teacher next saw John in April, 1981. He was still quite small for his fifteen years (5 feet tall, 89 pounds) but his pleasant, graceful manner had become even more pronounced. He made the teacher feel at home instantly.

143

School was still a place in which John felt himself to be a stranger. Although his last semester's grades had been good with the exception of algebra (Spanish—B, science—B, English—A, social studies—B, algebra—F), he had made no friends. The students smoked marijuana and cigarettes and drank beer, he said. His parents would never tolerate his participating in these activities, John emphasized, so he found himself very much left out. The students picked on him and formed tight, closed groups, "like a pack of wolves."

Again, John's friends and enjoyment came from outside of the school. His two closest friends (twelve years old) were members of his swim club and their parents were friends of John's parents. They shared their problems and gave each other advice, John said. John had become quite an accomplished swimmer; he had won two ribbons the previous summer and intended to swim competitively again this one. John's future career plans included either carpentry or business.

In December, 1981, this teacher spoke to John on the phone. He was now in the tenth grade in a vocational technical program majoring in computers and taking regular high school courses. His grades, he reported, had been good: one A, two B's, and three C's. His future plans were to major in computer technology, enter the U.S. Navy upon graduation from high school, and become a computer mechanic.

The teacher felt comfortable with John's career choice. One of his most disturbed characteristics had been a fanatic attention to detail. He had obviously turned that liability into a marketable, socially acceptable avenue: computer mechanics.

Matthew

This teacher first visited Matthew at his home in March, 1980. Matthew was much taller than he had been before and appeared to be in easy control of himself. There was no sign of the disturbed behaviors which had plagued and marred Matthew's personality the previous year.

At thirteen, Matthew was now attending a well-known private day school for learning-disabled students. He reported being the youngest member of his class but the best student academically. This, Matthew said, had aroused resentment in the other students and they regularly physically abused him. Matthew reported having no friends in school, but of associating with the many children in his neighborhood. His personal contacts sounded like healthy ones; his mother told the teacher that Matthew had had three girl friends so far that year.

Matthew was quite involved in several out-of-school hobbies. He went on neighborhood "digs" and found and had started collecting valuable old glass bottles and maps (which he kept neatly rolled in cardboard cylinders). He had also begun a stamp collection.

Matthew's drive for significance had not abated; he had only altered the direction of its focus. He no longer wished to make a career of the army, but planned to enlist for no more than two to three years after high school and then to study to be a doctor. "Why a doctor?" this teacher asked Matthew. "To make money and to help people," he answered.

This teacher visited Matthew again the following April, 1981. He was even taller than the last time she had seen him—close to six feet. He greeted her warmly and blessed her with his full, focused, completely sane attention for the entire interview. During the interview Matthew reiterated his deep distaste for school, saying that he had few friends there, that most of the students were too strong and tough and uninterested in learning: "I want to learn and get out of school. They want to smoke and hang around." Matthew associated with a few of "the good kids" which, he said, only fanned the rougher kids' resentments.

Matthew's academic life existed essentially outside of his high-school environment. He had enrolled in several fire-training courses in the local community college (for which he could earn college credit) and had been spending every free minute at his local fire station. Matthew showed this teacher three certificates signifying his completion of three fire-safety courses—one in Fire Ground Search and Rescue and the other two in Hazardous Material. His goal was to become a paramedic.

Matthew's program after high school was to (1) join a pay fire company in Idaho, (2) become a forest ranger at the age of twenty, and (3) visit Great Britain. Idaho appealed to him because he had once done a school report on that state. Great Britain appealed to him because they had been our allies during World Wars I and II; they had excellent rock groups; and Matthew is part British.

The teacher asked Matthew about his former intention to join the army. That, he said, was no longer part of his life's plan because it required a proficiency in too many gym skills that he could not develop. The only gym activity he felt competent in was rope climbing, which is central in fire fighting.

Matthew's hobbies had remained the same—bottle collecting and stamp collecting—with the additions of photography and listening to the Beatles (whose songs reminded him of "a long diary" he could understand). Matthew's friends were those neighborhood teenagers "who aren't getting into trouble."

Matthew refused to discuss his past except to explain why he had abandoned his identification with antisocial people and activities: he had been caught stealing for "the umpteenth time" from a local department store quite a while ago (estimated by this teacher to have been one and one-half years before), and had barely avoided being placed in a juvenile-detention center. That experience had made him switch his loyalties to the good: "I had to stop."

In December, 1981, this teacher spoke to fourteen-year-old Matthew on the phone. During their conversation, Matthew expressed an even stronger dislike of school: "I don't learn a damn thing." He had been getting beaten up "every month I've been there" by the tougher students who, he said, resented him. His total attention, therefore, had been turned to his course work at the community college: "I take every course that comes my way." Matthew's future goals were to become a paramedic, to work as a forest ranger in northern California, and then to set up fire stations. He had been working with his local fire company for several months as an active participant and already accompanied them to five or six fires that year.

Needless to say, this teacher was astounded by Matthew's return to sanity, his embracing of prosocial activities and people, his singleness of purpose in the pursuit of a life goal, his realistic appraisal of his strengths and weaknesses, his ability to focus upon and use his strengths, and his transmutation of a disturbing fascination with fires into a laudable career of fire safety. Matthew's strength of will is, to this teacher, his single most powerful asset.

Andrew

Andrew had returned to eighth grade in a regular junior-high school. This teacher called his new school in January, 1980, to ask about his academic progress and behavior. She spoke to a guidance counselor about Andrew's academic progress and to the principal's secretary (who was in constant contact with problem students) about Andrew's behavior. Andrew was doing quite well in both areas. For his first marking period he had gotten all B's and C's; for the period coming up he had received no academic deficiency reports. In addition, Andrew had not once been referred to the principal's office for behavior.

In March, 1980, this teacher visited Andrew at his home. He was as tall as she had remembered him (about 5 feet and 11 inches) but his shoulders were much broader. (Andrew's father told her that Andrew had put himself on a program of lifting weights.) Andrew's manner was quiet, reserved, and confident. He was pleased with his academic stand-ing, and sports were still his major focus. That year he had played on two championship teams: football and basketball. Now, in the spring, he had joined the track team. Professional athletics remained Andrew's career goal.

The teacher visited again with Andrew at his home in April, 1981. He was only slightly taller than he had been the previous year, but he was much more muscular. This time Andrew's manner was different. He had spent the day at a major annual track event at a nearby city university. Colleges, high schools, and junior-high schools from a large geographical area had gathered to compete; Andrew's junior-high track team had placed high. Andrew had spent the day in his element and was relaxed, happy unusually friendly, and optimistic when this teacher saw him. Andrew's father looked and acted genuinely pleased with his son and joked of Andrew's becoming a star athlete and supporting the family. He did, however, express his wish that Andrew would talk more.

Andrew reported doing reasonably well in ninth grade. His expected grades for the next marking period were social studies—A, math—B, general business—C, and English—D. His seasonal sports schedule was football in the fall, basketball in the winter, and track in the spring.

Andrew reported having one good friend, although he "hung around" a lot of people. His friend—an eighth-grader—was his closest, Andrew judged, because of their shared interest in sports. Too, the friend and he would talk to each other, give each other advice, and suggest alternative ways of handling a situation.

When asked how he had changed in the past two years, Andrew answered that he was more mature; he was no longer quick-tempered; he acted his age and considered himself to be "like a normal person." Andrew made special note of his recently acquired abilities to notice other people's moods and to change the way he related to them based on his perceptions: "I act in a different way." He summed up his life so far: "I've been through hard times. Now, if I keep this going, it's all cut and dried—no problems."

Andrew's future plans had not changed from the day this author first talked to him about such things. He still planned to go to college and to become a professional athlete.

In December, 1981, this author was unable to talk to Andrew. His parents, however, reported that he was "doing fine."

This teacher had, from the beginning, been impressed favorably by Andrew's singleness of purpose and unfavorably by his self-absorption. She was greatly heartened by Andrew's reported awareness of other people's moods and his adjustment to this. She hoped that Andrew's personal world would become even fuller and richer with his acknowledgment of other people and his inclusion of them in his life.

Thomas

Thomas had remained in Valley Brook in a loosely structured classroom situation. This teacher visited him there in January, 1980. Thomas was doing well. He had ceased his brutal violence and had been taken off medication. The most frequent comment this teacher heard about him was that he was the most mature, well-balanced member of his class. His present teacher was impressed with his intellectual quickness and with his ability to select a goal and to follow through.

Thomas was planning to move to a distant state as soon as possible to live with his mother, his sister, and his sister's family. He had visited them during Christmas but had, unfortunately, bullied his sister's children. As a result his sister was not willing to take him in immediately, and it was decided to postpone the move until the end of the school year.

During her visit this teacher noticed a series of pictures Thomas had drawn depicting the sequential construction of a building. It was notable for the disproportionately small size of the workmen in comparison to the building they were building and the materials they were carrying. To this teacher, these pictures signified Thomas's dwarfed view of people and especially of himself.

The teacher visited Thomas at Valley Brook for a longer period of time in March, 1980. His present teacher continued to express her pleasure with Thomas's self-direction. He had instituted an academic folder system out of which he assigned himself a certain amount of work each day. Upon inspection, this teacher discovered that this was the *identical* folder system which she had given to Thomas the previous year and which he had steadfastly refused to work in for the first seven months of that year. Thomas's present teacher also reported that, since February, Thomas had spoken of his behavior the previous year as if it had been that of a stranger whose motives he didn't understand: "I don't know why I acted like I did." He had just realized that his last year's class assistant (with whom he had had a year-long feud) had "been on him" because she had cared about him. Most interesting with Thomas's role of prosecutor in a class trial of a misbehaving student. His present teacher said Thomas had played his role well and that the student had been assigned a reasonable punishment by the class. In addition, this teacher noticed one of Thomas's drawings of a man climbing into a van. The man was drawn to scale.

Thomas was definitely to move in June to live with his mother, sister, and sister's family. His present teacher said he was apprehensive about the move; but when this teacher spoke to him, Thomas exhibited no apprehension or hesitation at all—he was definitely moving home.

In April, 1981, this teacher took a plane and then rented a car to visit Thomas, now fourteen. He was in awe of her follow-through and repeatedly said he "couldn't believe" she had come all that way just to see him. Thomas was now living alone with his mother in a spacious, nicely decorated apartment in a racially integrated apartment complex.

This teacher was stunned by his powerful, muscular build. (His mother told her that Thomas's father had been 6 feet and 9 inches tall and had weighed 290 pounds; Thomas, listening to this, was adamant that he was not going to get that big.)

Thomas seemed more relaxed and happier than this teacher had ever known him to be. He looked relieved to be living with his mother and told this teacher that ''I'm just considered a normal person like everybody.'' He was attending eighth grade in a compensatory program in a regular junior-high school, taking science, English, math, gym, shop, and track. He had quit acting out: ''I ain't taking tempers,'' and when asked why, said that his school friends had talked to him and told him his temper had to change. Too, Thomas reported, the school had stringent punishments for rule breakers, including calling in the student's parents and placing the student on in-school suspension.

Thomas basically liked school, especially track and construction shop. He spoke of its importance in his life: ''I want to be something. I got to have some kind of decent living. To do that I need an education, so I'm trying a little harder in school. I'm preparing myself for what I want to do.'' (Thomas had decided to pursue either carpentry or track as his life's work.) ''If I can't do it, then I'm going to have to take whatever's available.''

When asked to describe himself, Thomas said he was shy, quiet, always alone, and always walking. ''It gives you time to think.'' He reported having no close friends. The boys with whom he associated in school were not acceptable enough for Thomas to invite home. They smoked and drank, but, Thomas observed, they were active and they helped him to curb his temper.

This teacher and Thomas took the time to assess how very far he had come. Two years ago he would have been totally incapable of attending daily track practice or of sitting in and changing classes without a violent outbreak. He had mastered some serious deficits; he had a hopeful future. It was satisfying to this teacher to listen to Thomas laugh with joy as, together, they named his recently acquired social skills.

In December, 1981, the teacher spoke to Thomas's mother on the phone. The mother was delighted to hear from her and reported that Thomas, now in ninth grade, was doing fine. His school grades were average with the exception of world geography: special English—C, shop—C, math—C, science—C, world geography—D's and F's; and his behavior had not been a problem. She regretted that the teacher could not speak with Thomas at that time, but Thomas was attending church services.

It seemed to this teacher that Thomas's quest to understand where he fit into the universal scheme of things had been at least partly fulfilled.

He had found his home and, from that base, could safely travel the next stretch.

Philip

Philip had returned to the eighth grade in a regular junior high school. In January, 1980, this teacher spoke with a guidance counselor about his academic progress and with the principal's secretary (who was acquainted with the school's behavior problems) about his behavior. For the first marking period Philip had received C's in all of his subjects but English and reading, both of which he had failed. For the upcoming second marking period, Philip had received deficiency reports in social studies, reading and science. Philip had not once, however, been referred to the principal's office for behavior.

In March, 1980, this teacher visited Philip at his home. She was astonished at his height—he had grown four inches and proudly announced that he was the tallest member of his family. Philip was charming to the teacher, but he avoided talking in specifics about school. It was obvious, however, that school was a problem: as Philip and the teacher entered his home, his reading resource-room teacher called to report Philip's insolent remarks to her that day as she had tried to get him to do some work he had not wanted to do. Philip's mother's eyes flashed in intense anger but Philip quickly and calmly played down the call; the issue was dropped. Philip had continued with his sports activities. He was now playing on two baseball teams (one in and the other outside of school) and on the school's hockey team. His career goals, however, did not include sports. He had decided to work with his father. The visit was extremely pleasant; Philip went out of his way to be cordial and welcoming; but there was an underlying tension about school, which Philip was careful to avoid discussing.

In April, 1980, this teacher received a most heartening note from Philip. It read: "For my report card I got for social studies—C—science—B—English—C—reading—C—math—B. It shocked me! When I got home my mom and dad were very happy."

In April, 1981, this teacher again visited Philip at his home. He was now six feet tall and quite pleased with his height. School had been a successful experience this year for Philip. He had failed no subjects all year and said, "I can do that work if I study." His last term's marks had been average with the exception of algebra: science—C, English—C, algebra—D, social studies—C, general business—B, gym—outstanding. In addition, Philip had taken wood shop, guitar, and cooking. Business was to be his major. Philip was still playing on two baseball teams, one in and one outside of school, and said that sometimes he went to two practice sessions a day.

When asked how he had changed, Philip replied, "I've calmed down. I don't get mad that easy." He attributed this change in attitude to the strictness of the school system: they readily suspended students and called in the parents.

Philip reported having two closest friends. They were his closest, he judged, because they would do things together, such as play ball, go boating, and get up at 3:00 A.M. to watch deer in a nearby reservoir. Interestingly, Philip said that he was "willing to change a lot to make a friend" and that he had learned to accept a friend's criticism of him because, he reasoned, one must be able to take criticism on a job.

This teacher felt that Philip had finally mastered his overly personal reaction to things and had found a useful way (as preparation for success in the job market) to use the criticism he at one time could not have accepted. Philip's desire to have social and worldly success may have led him to sublimate the energy of those behaviors which had been blocking his progress. By mastering himself, he was on the way to becoming the person he had always wanted to be.

Peter

Peter had remained in Valley Brook in an excellent classroom situation. This teacher visited him there in January, 1980. Peter was doing well in school: his teacher was pleased with him; he seemed happy and content with her and with the classroom.

Peter's major problems were at home. His family had moved into a large apartment complex in another town and lived, as always, on the brink of poverty. Illness and accidents had plagued them that year. Peter physically shook as he spoke of his family.

Peter was interviewed again by this teacher in March of the same year. His family situation had deteriorated rapidly. Peter informed the teacher that his parents had separated and were planning to divorce. The relationship between Peter and his mother had become most difficult: he bitterly complained that she had been engaging in extremely socially inappropriate behavior and that he had been left with almost total care of his two younger siblings; on one occasion, he said, his mother had even failed to leave enough food in the house for the three children. Serious and violent confrontations had ensued.

As a result of these confrontations, his mother (with the help of Valley Brook) had referred Peter to the local state mental hospital for psychiatric testing. The psychiatrist had declared Peter perfectly sane, and had helped him and his mother set up a contractural system in which Peter would have his week nights free and the mother would have her weekend nights free. When this teacher spoke with Peter, he reported that the arrangement was working well.

During this interview (which was held in Peter's home), the teacher was struck by the strong attachment of Peter's baby sister to him. The little girl seemed particularly happy and comfortable when in his company, and she squirmed from her mother's lap to sit with Peter during the interview. At the end of the visit, this teacher and Peter left the apartment together—the teacher to go to her car and Peter to earn money by babysitting.

On February 15, 1981, the teacher received a long-distance call from Peter. He had had a final argument with his mother which had ended at the police station. His father had been contacted; now Peter and his two siblings were living with their father in another state. Peter was enrolled in ninth grade in a regular school and reported being quite pleased with it. His grades had been English—A, social studies—B, metal shop—B, wood shop—D, math—F. He was also taking Acting I and debating, which he thoroughly enjoyed. He had, however, disobeyed the directive of a teacher and had gotten suspended.

Peter's immediate plan was to enter vocational technical school the following year and to major in beauty and culture. His long-range plan was to work with mentally retarded children.

This teacher visited Peter, now living with his father, in April, 1981. Although Peter spoke of loving his father and of feeling good about living with him, family problems and responsibilities still plagued him. Peter's younger brother had struck his classroom teacher and had been placed in a special class for the emotionally disturbed. His sister appeared to be even more strongly attached to and dependent upon him than she had been before. Peter reported that she had been calling him "Mommie" and that it had taken all he had to break her of the habit.

School continued to be a good experience for Peter. Although he had been placed in compensatory math, he had earned A's in debating, had won a debating award, continued to enjoy acting, had joined the track team, and had definitely decided upon beauty and culture as his major subject.

Outside of school Peter was pursuing social-service activities: "I like helping people." He was a volunteer in a nursing home, where he talked and read to the patients and worried about their loneliness. He also occasionally attended a church with handicapped people and held their hymnals for them. That summer he planned to work in a summer camp for disturbed and learning-disabled children.

Peter's future plans were to join the U.S. Air Force Reserves. He and his best friend had sent away for information and were planning to join together. In addition, Peter had sent for information on a half dozen colleges and universities and had made arrangements to visit one of them in the next month.

This teacher was impressed by the number of avenues Peter was pursuing and with his generally happy and hopeful view of his life.

In August of the same year, this teacher received another phone call. Peter and his father were now having serious conflicts; Peter had tried to run away several times, but had always been returned. Finally, he said, he had dressed up in women's clothing to avoid detection by the police and had fled to his grandparents' house. His grandparents had referred him to family services; and Peter had been placed in a foster home of eight boys, staffed by one couple.

While Peter was impressed with his plush surroundings (a big house, his own room, his own phone, a swimming pool in the back yard), his attachment to his family remained paramount. He expressed concern for his brother and sister, who were now living with an aunt and uncle. He wanted to see them in a permanent home and hoped that they would not have the unhappy experiences he had had. "It's no picnic, let me tell you." Peter also declared his intention to save up enough money from an after-school job to return to live with his mother the following year. He intended to send his earnings to his mother so that she could put a down payment on an apartment for the two of them.

A few weeks after the last phone call, Peter called this teacher again to tell her that he had run away from the foster placement because, he said, there had been no adult control; the boys had been taking drugs and were pressuring him to join them. He had quit school and was now living in a juvenile shelter which he planned to leave soon. (Because Peter planned to leave the shelter, he did not give this teacher his phone number there.)

In December, 1981, this teacher tracked Peter down by phone and found him still living at the shelter. For the first time, he sounded downcast and listless. The adults in his family had made it clear to him that they no longer wanted him in their lives. His grandparents were disgusted with Peter's quitting school, his running away from the foster home, and his need for them in the courtroom several times. His mother had moved with instructions that no one tell Peter where she had gone. His father did not want to have anything to do with him. At the shelter Peter claimed he had been sexually assaulted by another boy and was pressing charges; the accused boy then decided to press charges against Peter. Peter told this teacher that he felt partially responsible for his family's rejection of him (although he did not detail his failings), that he was looking for some place to go, and that he had no money.

The teacher, an impoverished graduate student, immediately sent Peter twenty dollars (explaining that she would not be able to give him any more) and several books about finding the God within and from there contacting peace and contentment in the midst of outer storm. Waiting a few days, the teacher called Peter again—just several hours after he had received her package. By that time he had spent the money ("I spent it wisely"), read three of the briefer books, and was starting the chapters the teacher had recommended in a fourth. They talked about using devastating situations better to understand one's self, better to serve others, and to reach the unshakable God-self within. Peter seemed most grateful for the conversation and promised to consider reentering school, which had traditionally been a primary source of support for him.

Nicole

Nicole had returned to her regular-school district and was attending eighth grade in a junior high. The teacher called the school at the beginning of January, 1980, to ask about Nicole's progress. Her call was referred to the social worker's office.

As fate would have it, at the time of this teacher's call Nicole was in the social worker's office engaging in a temper tantrum. The school was in the process of sending Nicole home and of referring her for alternative-school placement. Nicole did not want either action to be taken.

The social worker informed this teacher that Nicole had done well in school for the first marking period. She had formed good relationships with her teachers and classmates and had performed reasonably well in her subjects (receiving B's and C's and one failure in English). During the second marking period, however, Nicole had reverted to negative, manipulative, very disturbed behaviors. She had cut her classes, forged the social worker's name on classroom release forms, failed all subjects, torn up the referral slips for alternative-school placement, and alternately asked to be removed from her home and decided to remain in it. At home, the social worker reported, Nicole had squirted the sneakers she was wearing with lighter fluid, ignited them, and walked around the living room in front of her father.

The teacher spoke on the phone to Nicole (who sounded truly shocked and embarrassed at this most unexpected phone call) and exhorted her to pursue a healthy goal without being pulled from her path. Nicole did not want to discuss her behavior, and the conversation was one-sided and short.

In April, 1980, the teacher visited Nicole at her home. Nicole was much taller (estimated 5 feet and 9 inches); her hair was longer and nicely styled. What struck this teacher was Nicole's quiet, ladylike manner. She moved gracefully and observed the social amenities—finding the teacher a nice place to sit, offering her something to drink, apologizing for the state of the house (which was immaculate). This teacher later found out that Nicole had been placed on Ritalin, an antihyperative drug. This would certainly account for Nicole's quiet manner.

Reminiscent of her former situation in the regular school system, Nicole was now attending the junior high on a half-time basis. She told the teacher that she was grateful to be in school at all and that she had fought to hold on to even this much time: "I made up my mind I was *not* getting thrown out of that school." She expressed a strong desire to return to school full time.

Nicole's future plans were to be a policewoman. That past summer she had done volunteer work at her local suburban police station and she planned to work there again this summer. With emotion, Nicole reported that the policemen at the station had laughed at her, saying that their force would never hire a female "cop." She had retorted by saying she would join a city police force if the local force wouldn't have her.

The teacher left, feeling that Nicole was a quiet, sad, and lonely child.

This teacher visited Nicole again one year later, in April, 1981. Although Nicole failed to appear at the appointed time, the teacher waited for her. One hour past the appointment time the teacher noticed a tall, slightly stooped girl with shoulder-length hair walking in long strides from side to side up the street. It was Nicole. Nicole offered no explanation for her failure to keep her appointment but immediately launched into a tale of someone's falling into a body of water with all the relish she used to show when something exciting or dangerous had happened.

Nicole had been expelled from the junior-high school and placed in the county vocational-technical school with the toughest adolescents in the public-school system. There, she was studying to be a health assistant. Her behavior in the vocational school had been such that she, with several other students, had been suspended for one month. "I like to wander," she said. "Wandering" had consisted of hanging in the hallways during class time and causing a commotion. At the time of this interview, Nicole claimed she had stopped wandering, had returned to her classes, and was trying to improve her grades of C, D, and F. She was going to do better, she asserted: "I have to change my attitude. The school doesn't really need any of us. We need the school. That's what it is."

Nicole still enjoyed baseball and basketball. Her plans included pursuing the health-assistant specialty in vocational-technical school this year, returning to the regular high school the next, and eventually becoming a nurse. Being a policewoman still appealed to Nicole because, she said, "There's a lot of action"; but she was not overtly pursuing that option at this time.

The teacher called Nicole in December, 1981. Nicole was a full-time tenth grader in the regular high school. She reported having skipped school a lot in the beginning but having dropped that activity because she had found it "boring." Her grades had been acceptable (B's, C's, one failure in English), and she had joined the basketball team. Her future plans were to become a lab technician and to begin training for it in a special after-school program during her junior year in high school.

To this teacher, Nicole appeared to have moved forward, although she had pursued many counterproductive avenues along the way. It was hard to imagine Nicole's finishing her remaining two years of high school without incident, but the teacher was heartened by the fact that Nicole had managed (at least to December, 1981) to remain in the regular-school system.

Follow-Up Moral-Judgment Scores

The preceding presented the students' histories for the two years following the intervention program. This section presents the moral-judgment interview scores for those two years.

Tables B–1 and B–2 represent the intervention moral-judgment data and introduce the moral-judgment follow-up data. Table B–2 gives yearly and overall change MMS scores. Although the experimental class had dispersed in 1980 and 1981, mean group change scores have been recorded.

As already discussed, the majority of the students entered the experimental classroom reasoning at Stage 2/1 and exited reasoning at Stage

Table B–1
Global Stage Change Scores 1978–1981

	Intervention		Follow Up	
Students	1978 Pretest	1979 Posttest	1980	1981
John	1	2/3	2/3/1	3/2
Matthew	2/1(3)	3/2	3/2	3
Andrew	2/1	2(1)	2	3/2
Thomas	3/2	2(1)	2	2/3
Philip	2/1	3/2(4)	2	2/3
Peter	2/1	3/2	2(1)	2/3
Nicole	2/3	2/3	3	3/2

Table B–2
Moral-Maturity-Change Scores 1978–1981

Students	1978 Pretest	1979 Posttest	Intervention Change	1980	Change 1979–80	1981	Change 1980–81	Overall Change 1978–81
John	120	242	+122	175	−67	265	+90	+145
Matthew	175	258	+83	260	+2	295	+35	+120
Andrew	160	185	+25	204	+19	254	+50	+94
Thomas	254	197	−57	215	+18	225	+10	−29
Philip	163	270	+107	210	−60	210	0	+47
Peter	160	264	+104	173	−91	214	+41	+54
Nicole	220	231	+11	290	+59	243	−47	+23
Mean	179	235	+56	218	−17	244	+26	+65

2/3. The first-year follow-up indicated that three students (Nicole, Andrew, and Thomas) had advanced in stage and MMS score from their 1979 posttests; three (John, Philip, and Peter) had regressed; and one (Matthew) had remained essentially the same. In the 1981 follow-up everyone but Nicole had gained in moral-reasoning stage and MMS score from the 1980 interview time, and all but Philip and Peter had progressed from the 1979 posttests. What follows is an analysis of the factors that could have accounted for the differential growth.

Andrew

Andrew grew steadily in moral reasoning over the two and one-half years of testing. It was not until May, 1981, however, that he used any Stage–3 reasoning. This use of Stage 3 coincides with Andrew's expressed newly developed ability (1981 interview) to notice other people's moods and to change the way he related to them based on his perceptions (a Stage–3 skill).

Thomas

Thomas steadily progressed in moral reasoning following his regression on the 1979 posttest. His steady growth in abstract reasoning, joined with his demonstrated long-term control of violent behavior and his mastery of the role-taking task, supports this researcher's initial hypothesis that the 1979 regression was a healthy merger of two disparate parts of Thomas.

Matthew

Matthew progressed in moral reasoning during the intervention year and continued to progress, although less dramatically, during the two years following. Most important, Matthew's serious emotional disturbance had been brought under control. It is this researcher's hypothesis that the exercise of reason in the class dilemma discussions was the wedge Matthew used to dislodge the block of his mental illness. Matthew had always possessed an indomitable will; he had always had a goal; what he had lacked was a connection between the two. His mental illness had, in a sense, diverted the energy of his will into destructive avenues.

When Matthew's interest was caught by the power of unraveling dilemmas in January and February, 1979, he zealously began to write dilemmas; three of them were discussed by the class. Upon Matthew's March reentry into the state mental hospital (where he had before been considered "their worst"), the psychiatrist was most favorably impressed by his willingness to work through ("unravel") his difficulties through discussion.

Once the connection between the will and the goal had been made, Matthew's disturbance subsided.

Nicole

Although Nicole had serious behavioral difficulties in regular school during 1979–1980 and attended only half time during the spring of 1980, she had progressed in moral reasoning. When this researcher visited Nicole in May, 1980, she noted Nicole's pleasant manner and age-appropriate appearance. Evidently Nicole had come to value the Stage–3 expectations of eighth-grade girls; this valuing was reflected in her moral-judgment interview as well as in her physical appearance. It is interesting that although Nicole looked and reasoned age-appropriately, her school behavior had still been quite disturbed.

Nicole's 1981 regression in moral reasoning (from 1980) is attributed by this researcher to her year in the vocational-technical school where she was surrounded by the toughest regular-school teenagers (mostly boys, probably reasoning at Stage 2) in the county. The hypothesis is given weight by the change in Nicole's appearance and manner noted in the 1981 report.

John

John regressed in moral reasoning the year following the intervention program. This researcher hypothesizes that his difficult transition into a regular public school was the cause of the regression. The Stage–3 familial relationships he had enjoyed in the experimental classroom were no longer available to John in the regular eighth grade.

In the 1981 interview John seemed very much more at ease with his lack of in-school social contacts (which he described as delinquent in essence). He mentioned two outside friendships which had probably provided him with the healthy interactions he had needed to regain his loss and to continue to develop.

Philip

Philip regressed in moral reasoning following the intervention program. Although he regained Stage–3 reasoning in the second-year follow-up

(Table B–1), he did not gain in moral-maturity points (Table B–2), nor did he reach the level of his posttest performance. This researcher can only hypothesize why Philip regressed and failed to make up the loss. During the 1978–1979 academic year Philip had demanded and received a great deal of this teacher's time and attention. He had inhaled the academic lessons and had earnestly participated in the class meetings and dilemma discussions, making great gains. In the regular-school system such personal, stimulating contact with an informed adult was not available to Philip; his environment no longer fanned his personal development as it had in the experimental class. In the relative anonymity of a regular junior-high school Philip, alone, was apparently unable to fuel the intellectual fire which had burned within him during the 1978–1979 school year.

Too, a strong characteristic of Philip's had been a drive to excel in whatever environment he was in. In the experimental classroom, the environment fostered moral integrity, Stage–3 interactions, and high intellectual achievement; Philip eventually excelled in these areas. In an urban junior-high school the male environment in particular fosters Stage–2 interpersonal skill; Philip reported no problems getting along with his peers there, saying, in fact, that he was willing to "change a lot to make a friend."

Peter

Peter, too, regressed considerably in his first-year follow-up and then gained, in the second, only half of what he had lost. It is felt by this researcher that Peter's loss of a stimulating, supportive environment and his catastrophic family situation were the reasons for his severe regression. Peter traditionally had had difficulties maintaining his equilibrium when isolated in his family environment for long periods of time without quality input. In the second-year follow-up Peter and his siblings had been placed in a healthier family environment; Peter's moral reasoning improved.

Discussion

In sum, environmental factors and/or peer interactions seemed to play an important role in the moral-reasoning performances of John, Philip, Peter, and Nicole. These students seemed to alter their reasoning in response to the environment in which and the people with whom they found themselves. This is most consistent with the behavioral patterns of these four students in the experimental classroom; all four had been especially attuned to social issues. John, Peter, and Nicole had formed a lasting Stage–3 subgroup, and Philip had sought repeatedly to unite the class socially. Andrew, Matthew, and Thomas, however, had always been more inner directed. During the intervention year they had never fully integrated with the rest of the class, and by choice. Their inner focus, perhaps, made them more resistant to outside influences; hence their uninterrupted forward movement.

Conclusions

The first-year follow-up interviews indicated that four of the seven students had continued to grow in moral reasoning; three had regressed. By the second-year interviews all but two had surpassed their 1979 posttests. Of the two who had not, Peter clearly and Philip marginally (Table B–1) had progressed from their 1980 reasoning levels, and both had maintained one half stage growth—a significant gain—from that of their 1978 pretests.

The data, then, indicate that the students who had been in the experimental classroom were continuing to grow in moral reasoning (overall change minus intervention change) and at an age-appropriate level.

It was not only in the moral realm that gains had been made, but also in the behavioral and in the academic. These seven students had been seriously disturbed for most, if not all, of their lives. (By twelve years of age, three had spent time in a state mental hospital.) Every one but Peter had been nonattendant in the regular-school system for several years by 1978; none (but Peter in third grade) had ever had a successful experience in the regular-school system. By the time these students entered this teacher's classroom in September, 1978, they were considered "hopeless" and there was no indication that any would be able to return to a regular-school system soon—if ever.

Within one year's time, however, four of the seven did return to a regular junior-high school; and three of those four adjusted to that system without major incident. The following year two more students returned, and successfully so. The one student who did not enter a regular-school program (Matthew) created his own successful educational experience by taking courses at the local community college. In addition, most of the students functioned reasonably well academically, indicating that the academic environment in the experimental classroom had equipped them with the tools necessary for competitive success.

The educational program in which these seven students had participated and the classroom atmosphere within which they had been enfolded in the 1978–1979 school year had had a generally positive and lasting effect upon them.

Appendix C
Student Compositions

Friday, April 20, 1979

Class Meeting

The things we worked out in the classroom were a number of things that we settled and discussed. I feel very free in a class meeting to say whatever I feel. Every week when we have a class meeting there are always problems to discuss and settle. Working problems out in a class meeting is better than starting to fight like everyone else does.

———Andrew

Moral Discussions

In moral discussions we make up stories which are about people who have dilemmas, which are problems that are hard to handle. We raise our hands to decide on what to write down on the paper. I feel deeply that moral discussions are a good way of handling problems. Moral discussions have about the same value as class meetings but we make up stories about people having problems in the discussions.

———Andrew

April 1979

The Class

I'm a lot different than I was last year. I learned a lot more this year than last year. My attitude changed a whole lot more than last year. My work has gotten better; my behavior has gotten better than last year. I'm doing harder work than last year and getting it all done instead of fooling around half the time.

I've got a more mature class than last year. If there's a problem they will sit down and talk about it. If they can't do anything about it they will make the best of it. In gym we play a lot better than last year. I got two better teachers. If you have a problem they will sit down and talk it out with you.

——Philip

Friday, April 20, 1979

Class Meetings

In the class meeting we discuss about what happens in the classroom and outside. We also discuss about how people in the class act and what we should do about it. We discuss old and new business and what we should do about it and what we shouldn't do. So far all the meetings have been going well.

——Philip

Friday, April 20, 1979

Dilemma Discussions

On the dilemmas we read stories and think about what we should say and what we should do if we were in their spot. Sometimes we fool around about it and sometimes we don't. I think dilemmas are good for us; it helps us think harder.

——Philip

April 20, 1979

Class Meetings

I think class meetings are good because you get to know other classmates better and you discuss problems. Class meetings bring the class together and help stop fights and arguments between the class. Class meetings help us all help ourselves. It calms me down and it lets us have responsibility; in other words, it lets the kids be boss.

——David

Dilemmas

I think dilemmas help us in many ways. They let us know what's going on in and out of the class. They tell us about the different races, like black and white. They show me it is not the color that counts; it is the personality and the thought. They help us not to put people down because of their color.

———David

April 20, 1979

Class Meeting

The class meeting is for problems that have to be worked out. A long time ago one person called another person's mom a name and that other person spit at that person. So, then, that Friday we had our class meeting and we discussed it out instead of fighting it out, and then we made a rule up: whoever called somebody's mom a name, three people had to hear it; and then they would tell the teacher, and the teacher would take points.

———Peter

Dilemmas

Our dilemmas are discussions about other people. When you are done reading them, there are questions to be answered; and when you answer the questions, you need your thinking caps! The questions are really good because you put your own words on it, and you can learn a lot from it. Sometimes they have things to teach you, like how to be "a little kinder than necessary" and tell about different people. You can draw a picture in your mind of what it's about.

———Peter

Friday, April 20, 1979

Class Meeting

We always would work out cooking and solving problems like when I started to be a showoff in front of the class, we would solve those problems. And when I used to pick a fight with somebody, we would solve those problems. And the things that go on outside, like, I would tease and fight with them, but we would solve them all. Now how I feel about them: (1) When we talk about something or about me the things you say would sink in my head and I would feel guilty about myself being selfish; my feelings are never hurt and (2) stealing, I would steal once in a while but it would only be like a candy bar or candy. I would try to stay out of the stealing business. (3) And other class meetings: I tried to get along but it seems like I'll never make it. When I would showoff in the front of the class sometimes I think I'm silly or dumb.

——Thomas

Dilemmas

There was never any problems to me in the discussions. But the stories were great. The stories taught me a lot—never to steal, never to get in somebody's business, never to break the law. I felt it really happened and it was up to the class to decide what happened to the person. And it told me what to do if I ever get in the middle of a similar situation.

——Thomas

What Is the Value of Class Meetings?

We have the class meeting so my classmates and me can talk about the things that are problems about the class. The kids would not be fighting because they would have the class meeting, and if someone would like to change a rule in the class they could talk about it. The class meeting made me mad because it took so long but it made me feel like someone, and it helped the class to get closer.

——Nicole

Dilemmas

I think the dilemmas are good. They help me think about how people like to live, and we can get right in the middle of the situation it seems. How I feel about picking a choice: It's hard because when you have a question like, "Should you let him live or let him die?" it's hard to give an answer.

——Nicole

Class Meetings

I think it helps people a little but not that much though. It helps stop a lot of fights. But when we asked Matthew to stop eating like he did he stopped for a little while, but then he went back to eating like he did and people got sick of it. When people got blamed for something they got mad at the person that brought it up. But it calms people down a lot of the time and it stops a lot of arguments.

——John

My New Class

I like this new class because the kids are my age. And I like the change. The kids don't get on my nerves. I get along with everyone in this class. I like most of the work. I still want to get out of this school and go back to junior high where all of my friends are. I changed a lot because I got older. I am ready to go back to regular school because my friends tell me about it so I know what to look for and what is ahead of me. The best part of the year is when I came to this classroom because I don't have to fight to be a leader in this classroom.

——Charles

Appendix D
Sample Quotations

What you are to be, you are now becoming.

Habits begin as cobwebs and end as iron chains.

A journey of a thousand miles is begun by a single step.

——Philippe Vernier

Habit is a cable; we weave a thread of it every day, and at last we cannot break it.

——Horace Mann

Our chief want in life is somebody who shall make us be what we can.

——Ralph Waldo Emerson

The only way to have a friend is to be one.

——Ralph Waldo Emerson

Kind words are jewels that live in the heart and remain as blessed memories years after they have been spoken.

——Marvena Johnson

We find in life exactly what we put in it.

——Ralph Waldo Emerson

The way out of trouble is never as easy as the way in.

One of the greatest lessons of life is to learn not to do what one likes, but to like what one does.

——Black

He who reigns within himself, rules passion, controls desires, and submerges fear is more than a king.

——Jordan

There's always a voice saying the right thing to you somewhere, if you'll only listen for it.

——Thomas Hughes

It is not what we have that is important, but what we do with what we have.

Every man has an equal chance to become greater than he is.

Every day we spend without learning something is a day lost.

——Ludwig von Beethoven

When it seems that everyone is standing in your way, perhaps you are standing in your own way.

Always be a little kinder than is necessary.

——Sir James Barrie

What is defeat? Nothing but education, nothing but the first step to something better.

——Wendell Phillips

The only way to improve our circumstances is to improve ourselves.

The victory of success is half won when one gains the habit of work.

——Sarah A. Bolten

This time, like all times, is a very good one if we but know what to do with it.

——Ralph Waldo Emerson

Character is a diamond that scratches every other stone.

Let us be the first to give a friendly sign, to nod first, smile first, speak first, and—if such a thing is necessary—forgive first.

Do that which is right. The respect of mankind will follow; or, if it does not, you will be able to do without it.

——Johann Wolfgang von Goethe

Old age, to the unlearned, is winter; to the learned, it is harvest time.

——Yiddish proverb

Caution is the eldest child of wisdom.

——Victor Hugo

It's not enough that we do our best; sometimes we have to do what's required.

——Sir Winston Churchill

The excellent is new forever.

——Ralph Waldo Emerson

When one door closes, another opens; but we often look so long and so regretfully upon the closed door that we do not see the one which has opened for us.

———Alexander Graham Bell

If thou hast gathered nothing in thy youth, how canst thou find anything in thine age?

———Ecclesiasticus 25:3

There is no right way to do a wrong thing.

Knowledge is a comfortable and necessary retreat and shelter for us in advanced age; and if we do not plant it while young, it will give us no shade when we grow old.

———Lord Chesterfield

Perhaps the most valuable result of all education is the ability to make yourself do the thing you have to do, when it ought to be done, whether you like it or not.

———Thomas Henry Huxley

Nobody ever finds life worth living. One always has to make it worth living. All the people to whom life has been abundantly worth living have made it so by an interior, creative, spiritual contribution of their own.

———Harry Emerson Fosdick

He who cannot obey cannot command.

———Poor Richard

Listen to learn.

Everyone needs to learn to stand fast under hardship.

Compare yourself not with others but with what you might be.

An informed and disciplined mind is the greatest asset a person can have.

The wise man looks ahead.

———Abraham Lincoln

He who cannot forgive others breaks the bridge over which he himself must pass.

Apologies only account for that which they do not alter.

———Benjamin Disraeli

The lesson of life is to believe what the years and centuries say against the hours.

——Ralph Waldo Emerson

Whoso neglects learning in his youth loses the past and is dead for the future.

——Euripides

Turn every obstacle into an opportunity.

It is an ancient saying that labor is the price which the gods have set upon everything valuable.

——Sir Joshua Reynolds

Give me a fish and I eat for a day; teach me to fish and I eat for a lifetime.

A person is constantly called upon to create his own future.

——Gregory Baum

People are in the fix they're in because they're the people they are.

If there's no wind, row.

To welcome a problem without resentment is to cut its size in half.

——William Arthur Ward

Guard within yourself that treasure, kindness. Know how to give without hesitation, how to lose without regret, how to acquire without meanness.

——George Sand

To reach port we must sail, sometimes with the wind and sometimes against it; but we must sail, not drift.

Shadows fall behind when we walk toward the light.

He that ruleth his spirit is better than he that taketh a city.

——Proverbs 16:32

Be swift to hear, slow to speak, slow to wrath.

——James 1:19

Lost time is never found again.

——Anghey

I can give you advice, but I cannot give you the wisdom to benefit from it.

Concentrate all your thoughts upon the work at hand. The sun's rays do not burn until brought to a focus.

——Alexander Graham Bell

To shield men from the effects of their folly is to people the world with fools.

——Herbert Spencer

What you do not want others to do to you, do not do to others.

——Confucius

The first step, my son, which one makes in the world, is the one on which depends the rest of our days.

——Voltaire

Patience is power. With time and patience the mulberry leaf becomes satin.

He who is not ready today will be less so tomorrow.

——Ovid

Argument thrives when facts are scarce.

Genius is wisdom and youth.

——Edgar Lee Masters

Nobody can think straight who does not work. Idleness warps the mind.

——Henry Ford

Seeing much, suffering much, and studying much are the three pillars of learning.

——Benjamin Disraeli

Life is a festival only to the wise.

——Socrates

An investment in knowledge always pays the best interest.

——Benjamin Franklin

Knowledge is power.

Chance favors the prepared mind.

——Louis Pasteur

Hear instruction, and be wise, and refuse it not.

——Proverbs 8:33

Shallow men believe in luck, believe in circumstances. . . . Strong men believe in cause and effect.

——Ralph Waldo Emerson

The secret of success is for a man to be ready when his opportunity comes.

——Benjamin Disraeli

Right and wrong exist in the nature of things. Things are not right because they are commanded, nor wrong because they are prohibited.

——Robert Greene Ingersoll

Happiness does not spring from physical or mental pleasure, but from the development of reason and the adjustment of conduct to principles.

——Arnold Bennett

Appendix E
Sample Behavior-Modification Chart

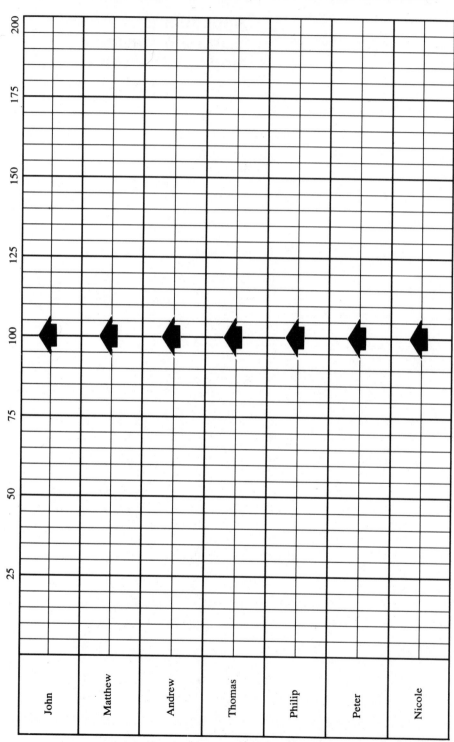

Figure E–1. Sample Behavior-Modification Chart

Appendix F
Moral-Judgment Interviews—
Forms A and B

Form A

Dilemma III

In Europe, a woman was near death from a special kind of cancer. There was one drug that the doctors thought might save her. It was a form of radium that a druggist in the same town had recently discovered. The drug was expensive to make, but the druggist was charging ten times what the drug cost him to make. He paid $200 for the radium and charged $2,000 for a small dose of the drug. The sick woman's husband, Heinz, went to everyone he knew to borrow the money, but he could only get together about $1,000, which is half of what it cost. He told the druggist that his wife was dying, and asked him to sell it cheaper or let him pay later. But the druggist said, "No, I discovered the drug and I'm going to make money from it." So Heinz gets desperate and considers breaking into the man's store to steal the drug for his wife.

1. Should Heinz steal the drug?

1a. Why or why not?

2. If Heinz doesn't love his wife, should he steal the drug for her?

2a. Why or why not?

3. Suppose the person dying is not his wife but a stranger. Should Heinz steal the drug for the stranger?

3a. Why or why not?

4. (If you favor stealing the drug for a stranger:) Suppose it's a pet animal he loves. Should Heinz steal to save the pet animal?

Forms A and B reprinted by permission: Ann Colby, Lawrence Kohlberg, John Gibbs, and Marcus Lieberman, et al., *The Measurement of Moral Judgment* (New York: Cambridge University Press, in press).

4a. Why or why not?

5. Is it important for people to do everything they can to save another's life?

5a. Why or why not?

6. It is against the law for Heinz to steal. Does that make it morally wrong?

6a. Why or why not?

7. Should people try to do everything they can to obey the law?

7a. Why or why not?

7b. How does this apply to what Heinz should do?

Dilemma III'

Heinz did break into the store. He stole the drug and gave it to his wife. In the newspapers the next day, there was an account of the robbery. Mr. Brown, a police officer who knew Heinz, read the account. He remembered seeing Heinz running away from the store and realized that it was Heinz who stole the drug. Mr. Brown wonders whether he should report that Heinz was the robber.

1. Should Officer Brown report Heinz for stealing?

1a. Why or why not?

2. Officer Brown finds and arrests Heinz. Heinz is brought to court, and a jury is selected. The jury's job is to find whether a person is innocent or guilty of committing a crime. The jury finds Heinz guilty. It is up to the judge to determine the sentence. Should the judge give Heinz some sentence, or should he suspend the sentence and let Heinz go free?

2a. Why?

3. Thinking in terms of society, should people who break the law be punished?

3a. Why or why not?

3b. How does this apply to how the judge should decide?

4. Heinz was doing what his conscience told him when he stole the drug. Should a law-breaker be punished if he is acting out of conscience?

4a. Why or why not?

Form A

Dilemma I

Joe is a fourteen-year-old boy who wanted to go to camp very much. His father promised him he could go if he saved up the money for it himself. So Joe worked hard at his paper route and saved up the $40 it cost to go to camp and a little more besides. But just before camp was going to start, his father changed his mind. Some of his friends decided to go on a special fishing trip, and Joe's father was short of the money it would cost. So he told Joe to give him the money he had saved from the paper route. Joe didn't want to give up going to camp, so he thinks of refusing to give his father the money.

1. Should Joe refuse to give his father the money?

1a. Why or why not?

2. Is the fact that Joe earned the money himself the most important thing in the situation?

2a. Why or why not?

3. The father promised Joe he could go to camp if he earned the money. Is the fact that the father promised the most important thing in the situation?

3a. Why or why not?

4. Is it important to keep a promise?

4a. Why or why not?

5. Is it important to keep a promise to someone you don't know well and probably won't see again?

5a. Why or why not?

6. What do you think is the most important thing a son should be concerned about in his relationship to his father?

6a. Why is that the most important thing?

7. What do you think is the most important thing a father should be concerned about in his relationship to his son?

7a. Why is that the most important thing?

Form B

Dilemma IV

There was a woman who had very bad cancer, and there was no treatment known to medicine that would save her. Her doctor, Dr. Jefferson, knew that she had only about six months to live. She was in terrible pain, but she was so weak that a good dose of a pain-killer like ether or morphine would make her die sooner. She was delirious and almost crazy with pain, and in her calm periods she would ask Dr. Jefferson to give her enough ether to kill her. She said she couldn't stand the pain and she was going to die in a few months anyway. Although he knows that mercy-killing is against the law, the doctor thinks about granting her request.

1. Should Dr. Jefferson give her the drug that would make her die? Why or why not?

2. Should the woman have the right to make the final decision? Why or why not?

3. The woman is married. Should her husband have anything to do with the decision?

4. Is there any sense in which a person has a duty or obligation to live when he or she does not want to, when the person wants to commit suicide? Why or why not?

5. It is against the law for the doctor to give the woman the drug. Does that make it morally wrong? Why or why not?

6. Why should people generally do everything they can to avoid breaking the law, anyhow?

6a. How does this relate to Dr. Jefferson's case?

Dilemma IV'

Dr. Jefferson did perform the mercy-killing by giving the woman the drug. Passing by at the time was another doctor, Dr. Rogers, who knew the situation Dr. Jefferson was in. Dr. Rogers thought of trying to stop Dr. Jefferson, but the drug was already administered. Dr. Rogers wonders whether he should report Dr. Jefferson.

1. Should Dr. Rogers report Dr. Jefferson? Why or why not?

2. The doctor does report Dr. Jefferson. Dr. Jefferson is brought to court and a jury is selected. The jury's job is to find whether a person is innocent or guilty of committing a crime. The jury finds Dr. Jefferson guilty. It is up to the judge to determine the sentence. Should the judge give Dr. Jefferson some sentence, or should he suspend the sentence and let Dr. Jefferson go free? Why?

3. Thinking in terms of society, why should people who break the law be punished?

3a. How does this relate to Dr. Jefferson's case?

4. The jury finds Dr. Jefferson legally guilty of murder. Would it be wrong or right for the judge to give him the death sentence (a legally possible punishment)? Why?

5. Is it ever right to give the death sentence? What are the conditions when the death sentence should be given, in your opinion?

6. Dr. Jefferson was acting out of conscience when he gave the woman

the drug. What reasons are there for not punishing a lawbreaker if he is acting out of conscience?

7. What does the word conscience mean to you, anyhow? If you were Dr. Jefferson, how would your conscience enter into the decision?

8. Dr. Jefferson has to make a moral decision. Should a moral decision be based on one's feelings or on one's thinking and reasoning about right and wrong?

9. Is Dr. Jefferson's problem a moral problem? Why or why not? In general, what makes something a moral problem or what does the word *morality* mean to you?

10. If Dr. Jefferson is going to decide what to do by thinking about what's really right, there must be some answer, some right solution. Is there really some correct solution to moral problems like Dr. Jefferson's, or when people disagree, is everybody's opinion equally right? Why?

11. How do you know when you've come up with a good moral decision? Is there a way of thinking or method by which one can reach a good or adequate decision?

12. Most people believe that thinking and reasoning in science can lead to a correct answer. Is the same thing true in moral decisions or are they different?

Form B

Dilemma II

Judy was a twelve-year-old girl. Her mother promised her that she could go to a special rock concert coming to their town if she saved up from babysitting and lunch money for a long time so she would have enough money to buy a ticket to the concert. She managed to save up the $5 the ticket cost plus another $3. But then her mother changed her mind and told Judy that she had to spend the money on new clothes for school. Judy was disappointed and decided to go to the concert anyway. She bought a ticket and told her mother that she had only been able to save $3. That Saturday she went to the performance and told her mother that she was spending the day with a friend. A week passed without her mother finding out. Judy then told her older sister, Louise, that she had gone to the performance and had lied to her mother about it. Louise wonders whether to tell their mother what Judy did.

1. Should Louise, the older sister, tell their mother that Judy had lied about the money or should she keep quiet? Why?

2. In wondering whether to tell, Louise thinks of the fact that Judy is her sister. Should that make a difference in Louise's decision?

3. In what way is the fact that Judy earned the money herself something very important for the mother to consider?

4. The mother promised Judy she could go to the concert if she earned the money. Is that promise something very important for the mother or Louise to consider? Why or why not?

5. Why in general should a promise be kept?

6. Is it important to keep a promise to someone you don't know well and probably won't see again? Why or why not?

7. What do you think is the most important thing for a good daughter to be concerned about in her relationship to her mother in this or other situations?

7a. Why is that important?

8. What do you think is the most important thing for a good mother to be concerned about in her relationship to her daughter in this or other situations?

8a. Why is that important?

Source: Ann Colby, Lawrence Kohlberg, John Gibbs, and Marcus Lieberman, et. al., *The Measurement of Moral Judgment* (New York: Cambridge University Press, in press). Reprinted with permission.

Selected Bibliography

Anne, Bruce. *Kant's Theory of Morals*. Princeton: Princeton University Press, 1979.

Besant, Annie. *The Seven Principles of Man*. Wheaton, Illinois: The Theosophical Publishing House, 1972.

Chandler, Michael J. and Greenspan, S. "Erzatz-Egocentrism: A Reply to H. Borke." *Developmental Psychology* 7 (1972): 104–106.

Chandler, Michael J.; Greenspan, S.; and Barenboim, C. "Assessment and Training of Role-Taking and Referential Communication Skills in Institutionalized Emotionally Disturbed Children." *Developmental Psychology*. vol. 10, no. 4 (1974): 546–553.

Colby, Ann; Kohlberg, Lawrence; Gibbs, John; and Lieberman, Marcus; et.al. *The Measurement of Moral Judgment*. New York: Cambridge University Press, in press.

Emerson, Ralph Waldo. "Worship." In *The Works of Ralph Waldo Emerson (In One Volume)*. New York: Black's Readers Service Company, no copyright date.

Frankena, William K. *Ethics*. 2nd ed. Englewood Cliffs: New Jersey: Prentice-Hall, Inc., 1973.

House, Ernest R. "Justice in Education." University of Illinois at Urbana-Champaign, 1975. (Mimeographed.)

Initiates, Three. *The Kybalion: Hermetic Philosophy*. Chicago: The Yogi Publication Society, 1940.

Irwin, Terence. *Plato's Moral Theory*. Oxford, England: Clarendon Press, 1977.

Kant, Immanuel. *Dreams of a Spirit Seer and Other Writings*. Translated by John Manolesco. New York: Vantage Press, 1969.

———. *Groundwork of the Metaphysics of Morals*. Translated and analysed by H.J. Paton. New York: Harper & Row, 1964.

———. *The Metaphysical Elements of Justice*. Translated by John Ladd. Indianapolis: The Bobbs-Merrill Company, Inc., 1965.

Kohlberg, Lawrence. "Education for Justice: A Modern Statement of the Platonic View." In *Moral Education*. Edited by Nancy F. and Theodore Sizer. Cambridge: Harvard University Press, 1970.

———. "From Is to Ought: How to Commit the Naturalistic Fallacy and Get Away with it in the Study of Moral Development." In *Cognitive Development and Epistemology*. Edited by T. Mischel. New York: Academic Press, Inc., 1971.

———. "Justice as Reversibility." In *Politics & Society*. Edited by P.

Laslett and J. Fishkin. New Haven, Connecticut: New York University Press, 1979.

————. "The Claim to Moral Adequacy of a Highest Stage of Moral Judgment." *Journal of Philosophy*. vol. 70, no. 18 (1973): 630–646.

Kohlberg, Lawrence and Turiel, Elliot. "Moral Development and Moral Education." In *Psychology and Educational Practice*. Edited by Gerald Lesser. Glenview, Illinois: Scott, Foresman and Co., 1971.

Korner, S. *Kant*. Great Britain: Penguin Books, 1972.

Leadbeater, C.W. *The Astral Plane*. Wheaton, Illinois: The Theosophical Publishing House, 1977.

Lee, Dal. *Understanding the Occult*. New York: Paperback Library, 1969.

Morey, William C. and Countryman, Irving N. *Countryman's Edition of Morey's Ancient Peoples*. U.S.A.: American Book Company, 1933.

Plato. *Gorgias*. Translated by W.D. Woodhead. New York: Thomas Nelson and Sons, 1953; reprinted in *The Collected Dialogues of Plato*. Edited by Edith Hamilton and Huntington Cairns. Bollingen Series LXXI. Princeton: Princeton University Press, 1961.

————. *Republic*. Translated by Paul Shorey. Cambridge: Harvard University Press, 1930, 1935; reprinted in *The Collected Dialogues of Plato*. Edited by Edith Hamilton and Huntington Cairns. Bollingen Series LXXI. Princeton: Princeton University Press, 1961.

Power, Clark. "The Moral Atmosphere of the School: A Method for Analyzing Community Meetings." Qualifying paper, Harvard Graduate School of Education, 1978.

————. "The Development of the Moral Atmosphere of a Just Community High School Program." Ed.D. dissertation, Harvard Graduate School of Education, 1979.

Rawls, John. *A Theory of Justice*. Cambridge: The Belknap Press of Harvard University Press, 1971.

————. "Kantian Constructivism in Moral Theory." *The Journal of Philosophy*. vol. 77, no. 9 (September 1980): 515–572.

Selman, Robert L. *The Growth of Interpersonal Understanding*. New York: Academic Press, 1980.

Spalding, John Howard. *Introduction to Swedenborg's Religious Thought*. New York: Swedenborg Publishing Association, 1956.

Stobart, Mrs. St. Clair. *Torchbearers of Spiritualism*. Port Washington, N.Y.: Kennikat Press, 1925.

Swedenborg, Emanuel. *Heaven and Hell*, 2nd ed. Translated by George F. Dole. New York: Swedenborg Foundation, Inc., 1979.

Vlastos, Gregory, ed. *Plato, A Collection of Critical Essays II: Ethics, Politics, and Philosophy of Art and Religion*. Modern Studies in

Philosophy series. Notre Dame: University of Notre Dame Press, 1971.

Wilhelm, Richard and Baynes, Cary, trans. *The I Ching*. Forewords by Carl G. Jung and Hellmut Wilhelm. Bollingen Series XIX. 3rd ed. Princeton: Princeton University Press, 1977.

Zain, C.C. *Astrological Signatures*. Los Angeles: The Church of Light, 1952.

———. *Cosmic Alchemy*. Los Angeles: The Church of Light, 1946.

———. *Esoteric Psychology*. Los Angeles: The Church of Light, 1937.

———. *Imponderable Forces*. Los Angeles: The Church of Light, 1973.

———. *Personal Alchemy*. Los Angeles: The Church of Light, 1949.

Index

About the Author

Eileen Marie Gardner was a teacher of emotionally disturbed children for six years and has been a student of spiritual laws for twelve. She received the B.S. from the University of Wisconsin at Madison, the M.Ed. from The Pennsylvania State University, and the Ed.D from Harvard University. She is now an education-policy analyst.